God Gave Me Beauty

Seeing *"Self"*
Through the Eyes of The Creator

Author: Dominique D. Harris

FOREWORD

Being a child of God, we recognize Him as our Father. God is our Father and a good one at that! In being a good Father, who resides in Heaven, God also gives His children good gifts or things as stated in Matthew 7:7-11. The key thing from this verse is not solely the giving of the good things from our Father to His children, but the asking of the children.

When we think about it, we ask God for a lot of things. Sometimes, we even ask God for things He has already given us, such as healing, peace and a Helper. But, what about asking our Father for beauty? Is this wrong? Is this carnal?

What is beauty by God's definition anyway? Do we have to do anything to essentially acquire beauty from God? Is beauty considered a "good thing" that our Father will give us? Is it wrong to ask God about our image? We often ask God 'WHY' He made us? However, we hesitate, ponder and even meander around how we feel in asking our divine Creator about 'HOW' he made us?

As we continue to follow Christ and mature in life, not only does our spiritual make-up enhance, but so does our physical. In the process of growing, we begin to notice ourselves and the culture of norms we live in. We come face-to-face with real emotions and are aware of physical deficiencies in all types of forms. Our adversary strategically places the demise of comparison to meet us in this process. If not intentional with seeking the Lord for understanding, insecurities can grow which may cause us to go into hiding, shame and even condemnation. How are we to live in a body within a culture that doesn't embrace our differences and uses our pain against us?

Ask and we shall receive good things from our Father, as Jesus taught us from the above-mentioned scripture.

This book will lead all those that are seeking for the "good thing" of beauty from our Father. Dominique has graciously written a guide and love-filled story in all transparency, honesty and truth of the beauty of God in us. Her pure intentions, hopes and promise is that she will lift up and lead others to the wisdom and knowledge she has received from past seasons of pruning and re-shaping.

God Gave me Beauty and Dominque's life, is a portal to help navigate others to another personality of our Redeemer, Jesus, and introduce Him as, "The Beautifier."

Ms. Janay Brinkley
Author of, "_God, Do You Like My Fro?_"
CEO of, The PushHer Project

DEDICATION

To My Mom,
"Thank-You" for doing it scared!
My birth is fruit of your fearless, "Yes."
You are a fearless, planted tree.
Don't stop pursuing the things of God.
Your life teaches me how to keep going!
♡ Love you ♡

To Ari,
"Little One"
May this encourage you,
to do what no one else has done,
the way God designed specifically for you.
May my transparency ignite a boldness within,
to share your testimony with the world one day.
Your transparency ignited boldness within me,
to share mine
♡ Thank you ♡

ACKNOWLEDGEMENTS

Khloe Myee:
"One Day, I had a dream. I saw a golden heart emerge from stark darkness. The heart belonged to you. The Lord showed me that He had created your heart pure, beautifully prepared by Him, like His Kingdom, a gift. I fell in love with God's vision of you. He showed me the kind of love He places in a daughter. Even in my mid-twenties, you were my very first reflection of God's love towards His daughters, from the beginning; literally, before you were formed in your mother's womb. You've shown me how beautiful we all are in God's original design."
1 Cor. 13:4-8

Dr. Jilliam Joe:
"One day, a lioness opened up her heart and her home to me. She then opened up her life and journey to me. It was the sign I needed from God that it was okay to trust her. As she took a glance back to see my journey was similar to hers in many ways, it gave me the courage to take a glimpse of my future through hers. Recently, I heard this lioness roar loud and spare not, and that day I realized it was 'UP' only from there."

Janay Brinkley:
"One day, the sun began to set. Darkness ensued. Before it became a snare, the Lord set His vision in you.
You opened your eyes and began to weep.
Now I can see, how His love purifies His vision for me."

Erica Callahan and also, To Tiffiny Martin:
"One day I walked into a room filled with far too many people for my comfort level. Expected to share what was hidden behind my smile. You pressed on my fears and it hurt. You called out my dysfunctions and it made me angry. You dug deep into areas

of my brokenness that others were afraid to dig into. You snatched off the bandages and said these wounds need the breath of God to heal. You didn't leave me alone to recover. You've journeyed with me the entire time. You've witnessed my transformation. Now I live… to press, call-out and dig in someone else's life. So that they live."

Tatiana (Tot) Jones:
"One day you walked past me shining.
A piece of glitter hit the ground and caught my eye.
It sparked a flame in me that had gone out.
It then became my new reason to shine."

Ivey Smith:
"One day, I had my head down, a bit discouraged with life. Then I felt a quick wind zoom past my face.
Going at a speed that allowed the wind to speak and say, "Your race... Your pace... Now Run'.
So, I ran. Today, I run fearlessly."

Pastor Linda Jernigan:
"One day I walked into a large room,
quiet and still, filled with hope and anticipation.
I calmly sat yet filled with anxiety... literally.
Afraid of things that no person should be afraid of, especially not the fear of man. I was! Then I heard a strong, decided, confident and courageous voice from the podium in front of me. Telling me about the 'Characteristics of an Evangelist'. You shared your testimony, your calling and God-Given Purpose. I felt your words unlock a destiny in myself that I didn't know was there. And as you poured out more and more, I heard God say, "I've given her the keys to unlock even more that's in you." Pastor Linda, you have been pouring ever since, and I haven't stopped growing one bit.

PREFACE

"The beauty that God has given us all,
has been there since creation.
It is a matter of allowing God to take you
on the journey of discovering it."
Author: Dominique D. Harris

There were times in my life when I repeatedly heard how beautiful I was; however, it was impossible for me to see the beauty others saw when I looked into the mirror. As a child, I was inundated with internal lies about my beauty which caused me to stumble into the world of comparison, which bred insecurity. Subsequently, by the time I became an adult, I was submerged into a full-on identity crisis! Uncertain about what truly defined beauty, and who I was, created an unquenchable inner thirst, which caused me to seek self-gratification. I sought love and attention in unimaginable and to some, unreasonable ways; that thirst for love and to settle my identity, caused me to make poor life choices. As you pore over the pages of my book, God Gave Me Beauty, you will read how I put myself at risk because I did not understand how beautiful I was in God's eyes.

Consequently, I penned this book, _God Gave Me Beauty_ because I found true, authentic beauty as a daughter of The Most High God! The beauty is that, in God's sight, I have always been His daughter and He accepted me as is. My journey consisted of allowing God to give me *His* vision that I may see myself as He sees me. My journey into seeing myself through the eyes of my Creator, has prayerfully become the means to unlocking yours.

Therefore, it is my prayer that through each word on these pages, that you will receive through Holy Spirit an impartation of spiritual strength, determination, and boldness to equip you for your journey. You haven't made it this far to walk away empty handed. God did not allow these events to occur in my life so that I can only look at myself in the mirror and think, "Glad you got me out of that jam." He delivered me from the clutches of hell, allowed me to be raised in an environment in which I would be given supernatural access and authority, in order to return to the place that attempted to take me out and free those who are still in bondage!

I am well aware that I needed to be saved from the life of sin that I was entangled in, but my awareness was heightened by the fact that someone just like me, who thinks they know God and His word may be falling for the same tricks of the enemy, which held me bound for so long; not because of what they know but because of what they don't know.

I pray, as you read these words, inspired by God's Spirit, that there will be a shifting in your life...Right Now! I pray that your thoughts are renewed...Right Now! I pray that there is an exchange of your will for God's perfect will...Right Now! I also pray that this book, _God Gave Me Beauty_ launches you into a focused, intentional seek for God, like you have never experienced before; this is my prayer for you. God Bless you.

Uniquely,
Dominique

TABLE OF CONTENT

"He hath made everything beautiful in *His* time: also, He hath set the world in their heart, so that no man can find out the work that God maketh from the beginning to the end."

Ecclesiastes 3:11 (KJV)

INTRODUCTION

Dear You,

You may have never heard of me before now, so, let me first start off by saying, "Hello!"

I'd like to share an interesting little detail about myself, which will preview the structure of this book. People who are familiar with me will testify that I have an incredible memory and an extraordinary capacity for detail. My mother often says, "You're the only person I know who remembers specific details about yourself at the age of two!"

Throughout my childhood, my mom always made the aforementioned comment about me. Unless it's something she'd rather I forget, then she says, "I don't know about that Dominique, are you sure?" We laugh because my mom knew before she ever asked the question that I am *absolutely* certain. She's really trying to figure out how I remembered *that* particular detail, whatever it may have been. That's our thing, it's what we do.

In fact, today it is a blessing because God has filled me with His Holy Spirit. My mind and imagination are the tools that Holy Spirit utilizes to communicate visions and dreams, hindsight, foresight and beyond. However, in the past it was what the enemy used to keep me in bondage. See what happened there? God placed in my genetic make-up, beautiful gifts to be used for His purpose, but in the hands of the enemy it became a snare.

Breaking free from the memories of past, traumas, and pain was some of the most extensive deliverance, I've experienced. That is the premise for this book; revisiting the past but not reliving it, for the sake of exposing the lies of hell and setting the captives free.

It is not difficult for me to remember things, especially life events because I process everything like a book or a movie. Words are pictures to me, and I can recall them like an index. Kind of like rewinding a video. Why is this important? Well... because of this, I have a lot of stories. Tons and tons of stories! I've found that rather than becoming enslaved by these images, with the help of Holy Spirit, we would examine some of these stories God used, as a way to set me free from the bondages of my past. In doing so, it is as though, I saw my past differently.

This book is comprised of many, mini-life stories; some short but others are a bit longer. The stories are not in chronological order however they do reveal who I was and how I found my true identity in Christ. I share these stories not just to reminisce, but to highlight areas in my life and identify where deliverance was needed.

I share these stories so that someone, who may not know exactly what deliverance is or may be blinded in an area of their life that needs deliverance can begin their own journey to be free—free, from whatever the enemy (satan) has crafted to keep you from your God-given destiny. For me, it was my physical appearance, family dysfunctions, pain, disappointment, sexual sin, addiction, loneliness and demonic relationships, and that is just the tip of the iceberg.

I saw the pain of my past as a curse. It felt as though I was not loved. It caused me to be bitter, resentful and angry; and, I viewed the world through lens of rage. My life was set to "Survival mode," and I was okay to just simply make it through the day.

I had childhood dreams, but they were dulled by disappointment. I was blinded by disappointment. I was afraid to believe because of it. At my lowest points, I'd given up on the thoughts of a future that I could no longer fathom. BUT GOD!

"And we know that all things work together
for good to them that love God,
to them who are the called according to his purpose."
Romans 8:28 (KJV)

A very gifted jeweler, who is also an elder and a friend, made me a bracelet. It has beads in different shades of blue (one of my all-time favorite colors), and attached there is a silver charm that reads, "Journey."

I wear that bracelet daily as a reminder not to forfeit the journey for the destination. The journey is just as important as the destination. Come along with me as I reflect on becoming the '*me*' God created me to be.

This book does to hell what it feared the most; expose its secrets! Many Christians do not like to talk about hell outside of their misguided attempts at evangelism. But it is simple, God has a plan for your future (Jer. 29:11), and hell's agenda is to destroy it (Jn. 10:10). Holy Spirit took me on a journey using specific stories of my past, to reveal the plans that hell had for my future.

As I allowed Holy Spirit to write through me, I could see how God's plans trumped the plans of satan every time in my life and in the lives of others. It is my earnest desire, that this book stir up a desire in you to seek God for His plans for you, and that by the end of your process, your vision is changed.

Godly perspective is the journey that I was taken on through this book. On this journey, I allowed God to exchange the way I viewed myself and my life, for His.

By the end, I found a broken little girl. I was then able to allow God to heal me, in order for me to begin to grow into the woman of God you'll encounter today.

Deliverance is a process. I invite you to journey as well, to see yourself, through the eyes of y(our) creator.

Chapter 1
God, "Why is My Skin So Different?"

<u>"SEE YA LATA ALLIGATOR"</u>

In 1988, at the age of four, I lived in Tampa, Florida. The neighborhood where I lived was predominantly white. I was in kindergarten at the time and our entire class met in the center of the classroom. We began to stretch out our hands to join in a circle. As I stretched out my hands, I connected with the girl on my right, but my left hand was left floating, feeling around for another hand and there wasn't one there. I turned to my left and saw the most disgusted face being made by one of the prettiest little girls in our class. She was white, but race wasn't the issue; my actual skin was the issue.

I remember it so vividly. She squealed,

"Eww! I don't wanna hold her hand! She has
ALLIGATOR SKIN!"

Even as I typed those very words, I remember the embarrassment of my four-year-old self in that moment. I remember feeling sadness, embarrassment, and isolation. We know that God does not desire any of those things for us. The enemy in that moment opened my eyes to the spirit of rejection. The seed of rejection had been sown into my life before I made it to the earth. The enemy is tricky and ruthless. It is my belief that that beautiful little girl didn't intend to hurt me. But the enemy used that little girl's innocence and ignorance as a weapon of attack against not just me, but against my future.

I questioned God that night, "God, Why Did You Make My Skin So Different?" God would later in life show me this answer in 1 John 3:1 (NKJV),

"Behold what manner of love the Father has bestowed on us, that we should be called children of God! Therefore, the world does not know us, because it did not know Him."

God reminds us that we are His children. He wants us to know that we are not rejected by Him. He calls us His very own. The world and those who love it, will not accept you or I, primarily because the ruler of this world is our adversary.

I developed eczema as a baby. By age 4, it had gotten worst. If you are not familiar with the condition, it is a skin condition that causes extremely dry, flakey and sometimes painful patches to appear on the skin. It shows differently on different people and different skin types. My skin was so badly affected that my patches were dry and actually scaly in appearance. I was so small that it covered large portions of my body. Consequently, we lived in Florida, therefore, her description of alligator skin may have been an accurate four-year-old depiction.

Remember, this story is not being shared to make you or I relive traumatic events in our lives to remain there. Throughout different phases of my deliverance, Holy Spirit has taken me back to places in my life. He has shown me exactly when the enemy planted certain seeds in my life in an effort to destroy my future. Not just to attack it. We must remember Jesus said,

"The thief does not come except to steal, and to kill, and to destroy. I have come that they may have life, and that they may have it more abundantly."
John 10:10 (NKJV)

Now what I would later realize is that the people in my life whom the enemy would use to hurt me, were just being used. Most times it is the equivalent to someone asking to borrow your car. If they commit a crime in your car, and the only identifiable evidence is the car, then you wind up looking like the perpetrator. However, once there is an investigation to take place one might find, that the driving force, literally, behind the wheel of the car was not that of the owner.

This is how satan likes to use people to do his dirty work. To be clear, some of that pain was caused by myself and decisions that I made. However, if unforgiveness and offence set-up in our hearts, it can keep us from loving and receiving love, especially

God's love. Without knowing the depths of God's love, it is not possible to know the fullness of God (Eph. 3:19), keeping us from knowing, understanding, believing or receiving, our full identity and inheritance in Christ.

This is no Christmas story, where the ghost of Christmas past comes to show you all of the horrible things for the sake of seeing them. Absolutely NOT! The supernatural gifts of the Spirit are tools that allow us to be properly prepared to face our enemy--the devil; and to have an advantage over him and the things of this world, like superhero powers. Because what does not kill us, we have victory over. God does not get pleasure from the pain in our lives. However, He will, if allowed, use those moments to turn one's mess into a masterpiece.

What I have learned about many people who are Christians is we love God, but we don't like to hate what He hates. People tend to cling on to the scripture that says God is love (1 Jn. 4:8), but not the ones that declare the things that God hates (Pro. 6:16-19). David says, Do I not hate them Lord that hate you? He says, I hate them with perfect hatred. I count them my enemies (Ps. 139:21-22).

The Hebrew word for perfect in that verse is *taklit,* which means completeness. Those in opposition of the Lord are also my own enemies. Demons are indeed our enemies. The devil is our enemy. We have to be bold in declaring this, because it has been our timidity towards demons that allow them to grow and thrive in our lives.

Because of this, we teach our little ones to embrace behaviors that are dysfunctional and opposite of their God given purpose. I believe this is the time when I began my loner lifestyle. If you know me now, you would never know that I lived a large part of my life identifying as a loner. People accepted this dysfunctional behavior simply because I put a name to it and claimed it as "Who I was." When I would disappear and detach from friends and family for months and years at a time as an adult, they would just say, "That's just what Dominique does."

I remember going home that day, after the "Alligator skin" incident at school and crying my eyes out to my mother. I don't have children, but I do have beautiful nieces and nephews. I've seen them all cry. I can only imagine what my mother's heart felt like to watch me cry to no end. My mother was a teenage mother, so she was in her barely, 20's at this time. I remember her embrace. She once told me about this moment, that she felt helpless. I could look back at that moment and say maybe if we would have prayed the word of God that day, the seed of rejection could have been choked out. In hindsight that may have been awesome. But that was not the case.

Somewhere there is a little girl trapped inside this deception. She needs *your* boldness to proclaim the Gospel as we ought to, in order to set her free. I know because I was once that little girl. My mother was once that little girl. Paul instructs us in Ephesians to put on the whole amour of God. This is for us, those who have come into the Body of Christ. We put on the armor in defense. He then instructs us to pray for one another. He instructs the saints to pray his strength to do the work in spite of his current situation.

"And for me, he says, that utterance may be given to me, that I may open my mouth boldly to make known the mystery of the gospel, for which I am an ambassador in chains; that in it I may speak boldly, as I ought to speak" Eph. 6:19-20 (MSG).

That then becomes the defense for those who don't know Jesus Christ for themselves.

"How then shall they call on Him in whom they have not believed? And how shall they believe in Him of whom they have not heard? And how shall they hear without a preacher?" Rom 10:14 (KJV)

The fact was, the devil had spoken of rejection, abandonment and murder over my life before I was even born. And although my mother may not have known completely about the full armour of God, like Paul spoke of, God never leaves us alone. He is always with us.

My mother told me once, how my father wanted her to have an abortion. I guess because they were so young. However, my mother told me of a conversation she had with God about me. All she said was, "I'm not having no abortion because I know what God told me about my baby." She doesn't remember what He said in detail. But that was enough for me to grab onto hope. Hope that God speaks to us. And with certainty that He designed a future for me before He formed me in her teenage belly.

Often times we go through life, not grow through it. I am a believer that whatever happens in life God can and will, if allowed, turn everything into good. I am certain of this because of one verse... Romans 8:28. Paul makes it clear that in all things God works for the good of those who love Him and have been called according to His purpose. Does that give you peace about your past? That verse brings me great peace about my past life and struggles. As a matter of fact, this verse will appear several more times throughout this book. That scripture lets us know, that although God may not have sent the trouble or the storms in your life (some He may send, Jonah 1:4) for those who love Him, He will take those troubles and storms and form them into something beautiful.

I am comforted today, and you should be as well, concerning your past. God knew that little girl would do and say those things about me that day. He also knew that my mother would not go and get her Bible and pray scriptures over me that night. And guess what? God *still* had a plan and His plan is STILL active, even right now!

I know for a fact that my mother loves God and I know she prays. She prayed a lot when I was little. I am sure because at four years old I found it normal to ask God, "Why Is My Skin So Different?"

God was no foreigner to me. God was and still is my friend. My very good friend and protector. I am thankful that even at seventeen, my mother started me on a journey of prayer and showed me the importance of a personal relationship with God. Just as toddlers do not typically pick up a book and say, "Hmm here's a good book that will teach me to walk." Neither is there a child that picks up the Bible before He or she can read and says, "Teach me to pray." But just as we model, coach and encourage children to walk and talk. We also have the same ability to, model, coach, encourage and/or sadly we can also discourage a child to pray fervently.

My prayer life started very early. Which as I look back on my life makes sense; because satan began attacking my future very early. The devil roams the earth like a lion, the Bible says, seeking whom he can devour (1 Pet 5:8). Who is more vulnerable than a child? God forms us with a great future in mind for us. In fact, He doesn't form us until He has a purpose for our lives (Jer. 1:5). Take heart in knowing that you have a purpose. But just as God created this prosperous future for your life, the enemy of your soul was waiting to attack it. Devised all of these tricks, attacks and distractions to keep you from pursuing the future that God planned for you.

You may be thinking; how did we get here? This story was about alligator skin. Well, let me continue the story to help make things a little clearer. That day when I came home from school, my mother admitted that she felt helpless. She then started doing research. She found a dermatologist who was doing a test on a trial drug on patients with severe eczema. It was an intravenous drug. Not like the topical creams that I'd been using. I pray the words that come next leap off the page, and you laugh as my mother and I do when we come to this part of the story. My mother said, days had passed since I'd received this shot.

One morning she woke up and looked over at me (I would sneak into her bed until I was about six years old), and she screamed to the top of her lungs, "Oh NO! JESUS! WHAT DID I LET THEM PEOPLE DO TO MY CHILD?!" By "Them," she meant white people. Being so young and away from family, my mother relied heavily on the community that was around her. They just all happened to be white women, also military wives.

In that moment she was in pure shock and anguish. My skin was covered in full on scales, scales and more scales. Not just patches like before, it was all over my entire body. It was so bad, I do not have pictures from that era of my life.

Here's the beauty. Over the next few days as my mother panicked and worried that she had made a wrong decision. One that would affect her baby girl for the remainder of her life, she would bathe me in warm water and would use only water. She was too afraid that I was in pain. I wasn't. I was itchy. She bathed me with oatmeal or something gentle. But over those days as she bathed me, she noticed that the scaly skin was coming off. Which freaked her out even more because she doesn't like to see stuff like that. What she noticed is that as the scaly skin began to shed, there was another layer of skin underneath, that was so smooth. She describes it as how a snake sheds his old skin and underneath there is that new smooth skin. But I'm a bit churchy and believe that snakes can sometimes represent demonic spirits, therefore I 'd rather believe of this time as God exchanging with my mother and I, spiritual beauty for our natural ashes; a real transformation.

God will take an 'ugly' thing
and beautify it…in its time!

Mirror Mirror on The Wall:
Time to Reflect

As I wrote this story about my four-year-old self, I remembered the embarrassment I felt. I remembered feeling isolated. As I wrote I realized that healing had happened because I could now see God's handy work in progress, rather than the resentment in my heart towards God for allowing me to experience this. Sometimes we hold the details of events in our hearts, minds and even areas of our body.

I would like you to write a goodbye note, to a memory in your past that you have held on to longer than necessary. One thing that has possibly been the cause of bitterness, offence and/or unforgiveness. This is a personal exercise, so be honest with yourself, this is between you and God.

After you've finished your note. Pray. Ask God to begin to heal you from this past memory and pain. I will also pray.

Father God, I pray that the person doing this exercise be loosed from the pain of their memories. And as a symbolic measure of ridding their future from the bondages of their past pains, as they throw out this memory, let it be so in the spirit, In Jesus' Name.

By doing this exercise it is my prayer that light is shined in a dark place, this is the beauty of deliverance. Becoming aware of darkness in our lives and allowing God to shine His marvelous light into those places.

"TURN THE TIDE"

Although my skin, after all of the shedding, was smooth and now beautiful. I would still have some adverse reactions to certain metals, fragrances, and chemicals due to the eczema. One summer when I was about thirteen, we'd moved back to Chicago, and I was thriving in my new neighborhood. We lived in an area known as the Near-Westside, I believe it's called the West Loop now.

I lived blocks from the United Center, attended elementary school near there and attended the James Jordan Boys and Girls Club of Chicago. I made a solid group of friends. I excelled above everyone in my grade level in school. In fact, there was only one other person in the school at my level academically and she was my best-friend at the time. I was feeling really good about what and who I had around me. I had community around me and I was thriving. There was nothing that could stop the level of ambition that I had. I had a boyfriend who I thought would later become my husband. Our relationship actually developed an unhealthy soul tie that would need to be severed, but that will come up again later.

I was involved in a young girl's ministry group called Divine Praise. We studied the Word of God together. We ministered the Word of God through dance. We were also fashion models. We hosted fashion shows and ministered the Word of God through runway modeling. The woman who mentored us actually started the group and took us to church with her. She was a woman with a past of addiction, who God had turned around completely. Through her gifts and talents, God used her to help guide us so that we wouldn't wander down the same path she did. She kept us covered. I know God sent her into my life as a way to protect me from all that the enemy had up his sleeves for me.

I was at a pretty confident place in my life. I was confident in God's ability and willingness to do everything He said He would. I was confident in my ability to do all things through Christ because I knew that He dwelled inside of me. The things that I mentioned before about academics, let us not be mistaken, I made it a point to give God the glory. There wasn't a test or homework assignment that I would do without prayer and there wasn't one that I completed without giving thanks. I learned the power of prayer through Divine Praise and my Youth Pastor, Pastor John.

It was the summer before I started high school, Whitney M. Young Magnet High School. A well-known high school in Chicago, known for its academic rigor. After all, our former first lady Michelle Obama graduated from Whitney M. Young. I was excited about going into that place and being a light. I was ready to get everything that God had to offer me in that place.

And out of nowhere, my mother switches laundry detergent!!!

WAIT! WHAT?! WHY?!

Yes! Due to my sensitive skin my mom had always used Tide detergent to wash my clothes. I could not use many products and once something worked, it was a disaster if changed up. I mean, I wore cloth diapers as a baby because I was allergic to any type of pampers. I wore stick on jewelry because I was allergic to several types of metal including 14K gold and lower which still has traces of nickel in it.

My mother not only changed from Tide to Arm & Hammer, but she went from liquid to powder. There had been a multitude of changes in our lives by now. One of which was my stepfather was now living in the house. They had been only dating before now and had separate places. When you merge households, things change; and the Tide was one of them.

I knew how to wash at a very early age and with the number of white shirts that my mother turned pink you'd think that I wouldn't even let her do my laundry anyway. There's another fact that I'm sure she'll dispute. But like I said, I rarely forget these types of things. Can you imagine, during an era where "white tees" were a staple in almost every Black teen's wardrobe male or female, what my face looked like when I found a slew of pink spots throughout my crisp collection of white tees?! Yes! I remember this very clearly.

Yet, some way she wound up washing up a heap of my summer clothes. I had my own funky style back then. Which was actually rooted in a spirit of fear and rejection. I'll explain. I wore rejection like a jacket so that no one else could reject me. I did the strange things that I wanted to do. Like, wore my pants inside out ironed to the "T" because it was intentional. Kind of like the group Kriss Kross wearing their clothes backwards. I've always done things my own way, but yet I was afraid that people would reject me because of it. Therefore, when people started calling me weird, I gave it a faux embrace. I would say, "Yeah I'm weird I know." When I actually didn't want people to call me weird. I wanted to be *ME* and simply be accepted for it.

That hindered the fullness of how I expressed myself. I felt as though I could only be the "real me" in small doses. Which when I think back, the very people who made fun of me for my style, would later copy it after a while. I wish I'd known the term trendsetter back then, because that is what I really was. I will never forget the day that I walked down the hall and saw one of the guys who had ridiculed me for wearing my jeans inside out, wearing his jeans inside out. But doing it with a way higher degree of confidence than I did and therefore, making it a thing, for a while.

I wore layers and layers of clothing. Layers were my thing. It was summer but I wore layers. I also, spent a lot of time inside of the James Jordan Boys and Girls Club, which we simply called, "The Club," but it had air conditioning. Although it was summer, I had on leggings, a white tee, and a sweater to cover my arms. One day, I got to "The Club," hung around the front desk, as I was often asked not to do and it was a normal day. I began to scratch a lot and I didn't know why. I carried on about my day. When I got home later to take a bath, I had small bumps all over my entire body except for my ankles where my leggings stopped.

I did not know what to do. I feel like I may have shared the same type of panic as my mother did when she saw my skin shedding as a small child. I retraced everything I ate, because I also had some food intolerances due to eczema as well. I did not eat anything new or anything that could have affected me adversely. I was not near any poisonous plants. We were in the inner City of Chicago we did not have to worry about those types of things. Crab apples were our biggest nuisance.

I took my bath, in tears, because this was a huge blow to my confidence. It looked like measles all over my body and they itched. As I went to get dressed for bed. I dug into the basket of unfolded clean clothes to find a shirt with a patch of caked up laundry detergent in it. That's when I realized that my clothes had been washed in the wrong kind of detergent.

I found myself questioning God again, God Why is my skin so different?" I wore long sleeved shirts and pants for the rest of the summer. I had gotten a topical cream to treat it, but it would take a while for it to heal completely. I was devastated. I did not want to model with Divine Praise during that time. I didn't laugh much. I didn't want to be around my boyfriend. This was a huge setback to the place where I thought I'd grown from.

Lack of confidence hung over me for the rest of the summer. It followed me into my first year of high school. Do you see where this is going? Where I had been excited and confident about how well I would do in school, I could not shake the identity issue that I had. What I now realize, is that my confidence was not anchored in my true identity. My confidence was actually anchored in my outward appearances. This happens when we don't deal with the fractures in our soul. We try to dress them up, hoping and praying no one comes along and calls them by their name. I remember thinking to myself, once it all went away that I was still cute, and that I had nothing to worry about but then comparison kicked in.

Here's how the enemy works. He has tricks, tools, and schemes to destroy you; well, he's really after your future. If he can deceive you into thinking you are less than yourself then you won't even think about the future. Why? Because you won't feel worthy to dream. Your physical man may still be intact; but if satan tricks you out of your identity in Christ very early, he can cause you to forfeit your own future by the decisions you'll make under his deception.

Sometimes Christians mistake the enemy for a dummy. I've heard people say, often actually, "That dumb devil." That couldn't be more untrue, the Bible instructs us to be wise as serpents and innocent as doves (Matt 10:16). Remember in "See Ya Lata Alligator" when I said snakes sometimes represents satan.

Yea there's an example; another was the serpent in the garden with Adam and Eve. If we are instructed to be as wise as a serpent, that means God is preparing us, NOT to face a dumb adversary but a wise one. Furthermore, Paul writes in Ephesians to put on the whole armor of God that we may stand against the wiles of the devil.

Mirror Mirror on The Wall:
Time to Reflect

In this story, "Turn the Tide", we see an attack against my personal and unique identity. At first it seems as though this is an attack against my social identity. However, when we ask God to give us new perspective and the mind of Christ, we begin to see things differently. My confidence was rooted in false identity, one I'd acquired from man. However, our true identity, is rooted in Christ. Apostle Matthew L. Stevenson III, writes in ABBA,

"God is the source of your identity not only as your creator but also as your Father. He calls you to draw your identity from Him."

For this exercise, I'd like you to make a list of things you've imagined doing but were too afraid to do because of man's possible opinions of you. It could be anything from, dying your hair that bright shade of red you've always admired on others, that solo trip outside of your country, or starting your very own humor blog. Whatever it is, make the list. Pray. Ask God for the courage to boldly be who He created you to be. And with God's wisdom begin to do some of those things you've desired to do. You may find that the you, you've been hiding is the person someone needs to seek their own God given identity.

If God gave you creativity, use it to advance the Kingdom of God. The same for beauty and fashion, sports, medicine, entertainment and education. Wherever your God given talents are rooted, be bold in them. Today is a new day. God has created us all to be ministers of the Gospel of Jesus Christ, you may not need a microphone to do it. Your tool may be a pen, sewing machine or a paintbrush.

Let's make this List:

1.

2.

3.

4.

5.

6.

7.

8.

9.

10.

Chapter 2
Who's the Beholder and Why is Beauty in *His* Eye?

"GOLDEN MAN"

Into my job walks this very handsome yet, very young-looking man. I did not look up from my computer too long because as I looked at his face, although attractive, I could not see past that baby face of his. He looked all of about nineteen and I was twenty-five soon to be twenty-six. To be completely honest, I should not have been looking at him at all. I had recently gotten out of a relationship. At the time that this very golden beautiful man walked into my place of employment, I'd only been living in Kentucky, for about five to six months. I had already been in a pretty serious relationship with a guy I'll call, "Superman."

When I moved, a singer had a song out called, "Superman" and it reminded me of him. Actually, it reminded me of a love that I wanted, and he was the person in that slot. "Superman" and I began dating before I moved to Kentucky in May of 2010. I should have known this was not a good relationship for me from the beginning, because I lied to my best friend at the time about how he and I met. I told her it was through mutual friends at a church but actually we met online.

The spirit of lust will have you lying to those you love, carrying false burdens, and accepting pain and hurt that was never intended for you. I actually think "Superman" needs to be unpacked a little more, so I'll tell you more about him in a story to come. But before we leave this place, the fact that I wanted him to be that Superman for me, to come in and save me, shows how broken of a state I was in. I had believed the lies that the enemy had fed me over the years and not held on to the truth of God.

"If you'll hold on to me for dear life," says GOD, "I'll get you out of any trouble." Ps. 91:14 (MSG)

I was calling this man "Superman," when I already had a Savior.

Back to the Golden man. Man. Men. It's funny that I had this infatuation with "Golden men." What that means is, a man with a certain yellow-golden undertone to his skin. Fantasyland was my home. I'd already planned out my wedding, already painted a picture of our home, our children and of course, the man who would become my husband. I had a picture of what our children would look like when his golden undertones met my red ones. They would be these beautiful Dark Brown to Medium Caramel complexion, very statuesque beings. They would be loved for their complexion, for their outward beauty and they would not feel enslaved by their skin. They would not feel like me; imprisoned by my blackness, even though I was made to feel like the beautiful exception to the, "Black is ugly rule."

I had made Beauty an idol! Shoot, I made beautiful men an idol.

Yes, God made man and yes,

"The LORD God said, "It is not good for the man to be alone. I will make a helper suitable for him"
Gen. 2:18 (NIV).

But there I was taking something beautiful and making it ugly. Perverting what God intended for good and turning it into my own personal idol. Kind of like how the Israelites did with the Bronze Serpent that God instructed Moses to make.

God wants us to enjoy the best things in our lives. How He goes about blessing us with those things is literally His prerogative. The children of Israel had cried out to God to remove the biting serpents that were attacking them, and He gave Moses a solution to their problem. He told Moses to cast a bronze serpent that if they were bitten, then they would be healed if they looked up to the bronze serpent (Num. 21:8-9). I believe this act of God confuses some Christians. Probably because we try to put God into this pretty box that should be packaged nice and neat and perfect. But God is Sovereign. What God intended as a solution to their problem, they later turned into an idol and began to worship it.

God gave man, a helper as a solution to what He deemed a problem. He said man was not suited to be alone. He wasn't built to live this life without a helper. However, God didn't intend for the man to worship the woman or woman to worship the man. And if I can remain very honest, I worshiped man. It went deeper than I thought. I used to give God all of His props on the creation of the male physique. Probably, too much! That spirit called, "Lust" had me wildin' out. I thought it was just physical, but what I learned is that I made God have to consult with every man I ever dated, in order to get to my heart.

When I told my best friend at the time about this Golden Man that I had just recently started to date, she said, "I'll meet him. Bring him to church;" so I did. It was a set up. I knew he did not 'do church,' but the fact that he said he was willing to make an exception for me made me feel like a Queen. He was born in Alaska raised on a Native American reservation in one of the Dakotas, a part of the Sioux Tribe. He did not believe in God, but rather spirits and nature and things that I would just ignore because we were not equally yoked, but he was fine! Fine as in beautiful!

He came to church with me. After the church service my friend said, "He is not the one." Offended, I asked, "Why would you say that?" She then explained how she'd watched me here and there in service. How I attended to him and tried to make him comfortable but how I didn't worship the way that I normally would. I did not focus on the word the way I normally would. Her description of that day sums up my relationship with God whenever a man was in my life. I'd drop the affections of God and advert my attention to whatever man was there. I tended to his needs, his feelings, his likes and dislikes, his physical needs, but I was not concerned with the health of his soul. Heck, my own soul was fractured in so many places, there was no room for the type of healing that needed to happen. I had refused to create that space. Jumping from one relationship to another, allowed me the opportunity to avoid the places in my soul that needed healing.

I really took my friends words as envy and not as love or wisdom. I'd actually felt that our friendship shifted in that moment. Me not hanging on to God's truth about my beauty, my worth and my identity in Christ skewed my vision of my friends and myself. I thought she just didn't want me to be happy. Bear in mind she'd just given birth to my Goddaughter. She had someone to love and who would love her in return, and I felt that she didn't desire the same thing for me. These were just lies. However, I believed them. Because I had rejected truth.

That same Sunday evening my Golden Man helped me move from one end of town to the other. It was only right, at least in my brokenness, that we "Christened the crib." To those who don't know what that means. We, so called, "Blessed" my new apartment by having sex right in the middle of the living room. Again, allow me to point out the perversion of the words "Christened" and "blessed" as a way to describe such sexual sin; fornication. In a religious context, those acts are Holy sacraments, sacred acts, a form of worship if you will. However, I didn't make them up, but these were very acceptable terms to use to describe what we did according to our culture. In our cultural context those were joking terms for a very serious matter.

I did say, he didn't believe in God but rather he believed in spirits and the universe as being all powerful. One way that he believed people to communicate to some spirits were through sex. I was not aware of the dangers of engaging in this type of sexual practice. I did not know about any of this idol or cultic worship. I am not sure that he fully did either. Did I have a problem with lust, fornication and sexual sin, yes! However, that was an open door for what I wasn't aware of, I was unaware that it was idolatry. Until a couple of years ago when I began going through my initial deliverance process.

But the Bible, the Word of God, God Himself warns us of sexual worship and cultic worship in the Old Testament. I believed that I *knew* the Word of God. But this was right there in the Bible. God warns us that whole nations of people like the Canaanites needed to be completely obliterated because they were worshiping Molech. God set Israel apart and gave them authority to overtake the Canaanites so as to not adopt their cultic sexual worship practices. As I even write this

I am blown away. All along, the Word of God was there in a book but not in my heart.

Golden man, introduced me to tantric sex. Practiced by Hindus, who believe in multiple gods (Polytheism). The word *tantra* means, woven or loom; Hindu and Buddhist ritual doctrine. Merriam defines it as, "one of the later Hindu or Buddhist scriptures dealing especially with techniques and rituals including meditative and sexual practices;" Y'all the devil was ready to set 'ya' girl up. All because I had run and hid myself from the truth.

Tantra is not only meditative sexual practices. I am about to make somebody mad, mainly the devil, but Yoga is also a form of this type of meditative indoctrination. There are more and more occult practices that many of us have been desensitized to mainly through media and social media. There is now a growing number of Christians in these areas of influence because the lack of information in my opinion allows many to keep an open door to the dealings of witchcraft and the occult. The word of God is powerful, and yet powerless if not applied in our lives.

"I have hidden your word in my heart
that I might not sin against you"
Ps. 119:11 (NIV)

Because I had not hidden the Word of God in my heart, I did not have the wisdom to discern good from evil (Pro 2:10-12).

But solid food belongs to those who are of full age, *that is,* those who by reason of use have their senses exercised to discern both good and evil (Hebrews 5:14).

Satan banks on this. What? No, Who? Is the better question. He banks on Christians who feel so untouchable because they've memorized The Lord's Prayer, "God hasn't given us a spirit of fear" and "I can do all things through Christ who strengthens me." He banks on our ignorance. We like to jump in and out of bed with religion and call it "Salvation." Making sure we hit up church every Easter, Christmas and Mother's Day for a few of us who feel like "It's the least we can do."

The whole time, we are as part-time with God as a sixteen-year old who works at McDonald's. Coming up with excuses as to why you can't make it in to work, simply because a friend is having a party that you don't want to miss. Only putting in the time to get a paycheck, not because there's any real commitment or joy in doing the job. And I don't know the last time you've visited a McDonald's, but the Calvin of the 1990's McDonald's commercials does not exist. I mean the McDonald's workers I've experienced in my past were more like, "Hey! Why you show up at MY window today? I'm not trying to do any work for real." This is how we have been known to treat our relationships with God. In it only for the benefit of receiving a blessing or something in return. Wanting to put on the uniform and name tag that says you're a Christian but not wanting to work when you're put on the schedule. Making excuses as to why you can't do what God asks when it interferes with the demons you don't want to let go, and treating God's people, those who He sends to you like they've done something wrong by expecting to experience God when they "pull up to your window." I mean your name tag does say "Hi, I am a Christian," *right*?

You may be wondering where exactly is this going? I pray, it's going into your thoughts and heart. See, Golden Man was an earthly vessel. As vessels we have the capability to be used by whomever. Whether, God, Satan or our own carnal soul. There is no doubt that he was sent to me. But from whom, is the question I didn't even know to ask. I didn't know that a good-looking man, I mean every physical feature that I've ever dreamt or prayed about, could be sent by anyone outside of God. He didn't even smoke nothing or drink alcohol. Still, I didn't know that, the kind, loving and patient man, that I prayed for could be sent from anyone other than God. I simply didn't know. I believe we make moves in life, as if we don't care because we simply don't know.

I am sure that this is why God placed this assignment in my heart. Back then, I legitimately believed in God and believed that was enough to sustain my soul. However, my addiction to satisfy my flesh through sex, marijuana and alcohol, were clear indicators that I was indeed missing something else in my life. This void would only be filled when I would eventually have a face-to-face encounter with God Himself.

Subsequently, at the moment when Golden Man and I were in a relationship I had not truly experienced God's love, because there were areas of my life, like relationships, that I had blocked Him out of. We tend to do this a lot as Christians. However, that is the very key that gives satan access. See, God desires us to come to Him freely. He gives us the option to choose Him. The devil more so, seeks access. He is legalistic in nature. Jesus will knock and wait on your response. Satan looks for a crack in the door and sneaks in. And any place that we don't allow Jesus to Lord over, we in turn give the enemy permission to wreak havoc.

"Behold, I stand at the door, and knock: if any man hear my voice, and open the door, I will come in to him, and will sup with him, and he with me."
Rev. 3:20 (KJV)

Some tests are allowed by God we have seen this in scripture in Job and in Luke when Jesus told Peter that the enemy sought to sift him. I am saying this for you to bear in mind, God is in control over ALL. And to remind us, that whether or not the tests and trials were schemes and attacks from the enemy or whether they were in fact tests sent from God, God is in control of it all. We are assured this in Romans 8:28. Whatever the enemy intends for evil God can and will, once we submit ourselves to His will and His purpose, work all things together for our good. But there first needs to be a decision made to follow Christ. I needed to make that clear. Not only is it important to know the word of God, it is important to also know what the prerequisites are. We must decide a life in Christ; that's prerequisite number one. Decide!

I need to explain that this was not just some random relationship. These sexual practices brought us into a space spiritually that was illegal. I would say I felt the most tormented in this relationship. Here's what I've learned, if you engage in anything that opposes your beliefs, that's a set up for torment. I'll continue so that you see why. Golden Man and I continued our sexual relationship for months until one day as I'm lying in his bed, I found my physical body literally craving to be with his. I remember having the thought like "Yo! This is crazy." He'd only gone out to get donuts and bagels but when he returned, I had a conversation with him about how I wanted to, moving forward, refrain from having sexual intercourse. Surprisingly, he agreed. I was shocked, relieved and now even more entangled in this web of deceit. His response made me "Fall in love" with him even more.

After making this decision, we continued dating, which was great, but we would begin to practice tantric breathing exercises more and more. Sometimes we would sit in bed face to face and practice sharing a breath. That was now our new thing. I can share now that I am free from this wicked soul-tie that there were times where I'd began to prefer to just sin the good old-fashioned way because this, what we had embarked on left impressions in my heart, soul, mind and thoughts that brought so much conflict in my heart and soul. It brought so much conflict with what I had learned of holiness and what I was actually feeling. Holiness meant no sex before marriage. This was what I was taught growing up. Fine, I stopped having sex with this man and partook in a whole other kind of pool of sinful acts. This is why I referred to the torment I felt in this relationship. I was taught only examples of sin, not given a true definition of sin. Although, I was not having intercourse any longer, what we were doing instead, felt just as bad.

Keep in mind whatever draws your soul from God is sin… for YOU!

Think about the Prophet Isaiah, he says, "my soul have I desired thee in the night…" David says in Psalms 63,

"O God, thou art my God; early will I seek thee: my soul thirsteth for thee, my flesh longeth for thee in a dry and thirsty land, where no water is"

Today I am able to read the scriptures and understand the depth of their longing for God to fill these places in their souls. But back then I didn't even know fully what my soul was. I knew we had a soul, but I didn't understand the workings of the soul. I now understand why I felt so empty and why I allowed this man and many others to fill the hole and emptiness I felt.

There was no physical intercourse so as a Christian I was cool. According to what I had been taught, I was not sinning. Wrong! Yet I recall a time where my best friend, who covered me in prayer, would later come to me and address my involvement with this guy. Again, I thought she was jealous but I trusted the God in her. Golden man and I actually broke things off, for years. However, during those initial weeks of separation I'd sent text messages wanting to meet with him and explain what I was going through. He never responded. He apparently got a new phone.

I believe that a part of my ignorance as a believer came down the pipeline of lukewarm Christianity. Those who told me that all it takes is that you believe in your heart and confess with your mouth that Jesus died and rose for my sins but that's just the beginning, that's Salvation.

Salvation is accessible for everyone. But I needed to know how to walk with Jesus like the 12. I needed to be taught the ways of Christ by example like Jesus did with the 12. The Bible says, they were *made* into

Apostles. Made, means to be formed in a particular process. I don't question God's ways. He obviously knew what it would take for me to turn to Him in complete submission. But getting to this place in the manner in which I did, is not what God wants for everyone. God instructs the twelve to then go out and make disciples (Matt 28:19-20).

Nineteen months later, 'Golden Man' reached out to me saying he'd gotten a new phone recently and when attempting to back up his phone all of these old texts appeared. Whether it was true or not I believed him.

January 2015, as I was about to complete my degree he and I began talking again. I started skipping classes to be with him before he'd have work and of course I was lying to everyone around me. I had grown so much in my spiritual walk with Christ by this time. I felt strong in my ability to make wise decisions but without healing those fractures in my soul and merely suppressing the feelings I hadn't yet addressed; seeing his face brought back a flood of emotions that I was not equipped to deal with.

One day, I laid with him on his sofa. How I wound up there was crazy. I recall a bunch of driving here and there, it was very chaotic. I had things to do he was now a father so he had to drop off his daughter, and he decided to play hooky from work. In his place we found ourselves laughing and joking like old times. We were very good friends and that's what brought me back in close. My best friend and I although still in one another's lives, would have our times of separation. Her and I were living together at this time, but we would have our good times and not so good times.

During this time, I felt super lonely. Loneliness was something that seemed to follow me throughout my life back then. I would later realize that it was indeed an open door that gave the enemy access to my desires.

Therefore, as we lay on his sofa after laughing dancing and playing around, he would lay, back against sofa my back against his, facing the television and slowly he began to breathe. Like clockwork, my breath met his and became one breath. He placed his hand on my stomach and without any sexual intercourse we found ourselves in a very euphoric place.

Later that night, I was overcome with guilt and shame. Let me tell you, it was all God that gave me the strength to make this next move. I broke things off with him once again. This time I went through a mourning period because I felt like no one would ever love me as deeply as I believed he did. He marveled at my beauty! I wondered, would anyone else *ever* see me as beautiful?

This soul-tie was one that kept me from receiving Father's pure love. I had entered into an illegal covenant with Golden Man. I believe many women and men need to know that covenants are binding. Many need to be aware of what soul-ties are. Many need to be aware that there are Godly ones such as God and His children, Christ and the Church, husband and wife and even friends like Jonathan and David. These covenant agreements are between two with Christ at the center.

However, what Golden Man and I had, had usurped the authority of Christ and went about establishing a covenant void of Christ. This is how the enemy perverts what God has deemed beautiful. Genesis 2 and referenced throughout the NT, God desires for two to become one flesh under the protective covering of covenant. There should not be shame and guilt in a Godly covenant. We see this shortly after in Genesis 3, the fall of man removes him from the protective covering of God's covenant. God establishes another but only after the first had been broken.

Today, I live on the breath of God. In covenant with my Father as His daughter. It took much crushing to get to this place. So please, be patient with your process.

I have no doubt been *made* into the woman of God that I am today by going through various processes. This relationship and others in my past were only possible because I was in so much pain. I viewed life through a broken lens. But when I took those broken pieces to the Master, God, Abba, and said "Daddy... here fix it." That process of healing is what has allowed me to see the beauty in every aspect of my life. Heck, I see the beauty in myself.

It is my prayer that this book helps you discover your God given beauty as well. I am reminded of a song that Leon Timbo sings. The lyrics say, "I lean not on my own understanding. My life is in the hands of the maker of Heaven. And I give it all to you God, trusting that you'll make something beautiful out of me." This song takes me straight into a place of worship. Because that is exactly what I did. I gave it all to God. That is one of the most powerful weapons we can use against the enemy. It is also one of the most beautiful features of our Father God (Matt. 11:25-30, 1 Pet. 5:7).

God *gave* me beauty, it is literally in my genetic makeup; but I had yet to learn what that looked like on me.

Mirror Mirror on The Wall:
Time to Reflect

Through this story, I learned many lessons. The spirit of rejection had me in deception, lust, perversion, and idolatry. But these things have one thing in common, perspective. Because I had rejected God's truth, and this is obvious because I had succumbed to the lies of the enemy. What lies? The ones that said my body was my own which gave me permission to do with it as I pleased. That is how lust ate supper hourly, not just daily.

The deception of believing I was my own woman made me feel like I could have and do just about anything I wanted to do. I was afraid of being alone, of not being loved and of being abandoned. As a result, I sought out counterfeit love because it was the only tangible love I knew back then. Our eyes are a gateway to lust. That is why our hearts have to be anchored in the Word, in Truth. My heart was the source of idolatry. It is in my heart that I removed God from the top spot and placed any man who showed the type of affection I was seeking.

Take this time to take a heart survey. I believe that this is an ongoing process, that needs the help of Holy Spirit. This is a process. What I have learned is that, God will create specific situations around you, that will in-turn expose what's in your heart. For example, you may feel like, my heart is good. Until your bestie who has been single along with you, starts dating a new guy and your heart's response is other than genuinely happy for her.

Therefore, this reflection is more on-going than the others. But submit your heart for examination. And allow God to show you how to deal with what is revealed.

"GOD IS THE BEHOLDER OF BEAUTY"

I had not committed the truth in my heart. But what is the truth? Who is the beholder? And why is beauty in *his* eye? It's in *his* eye, because that's how He (God) designed. Then God said, "Let Us make man in Our image, according to Our likeness; let them have dominion over the fish of the sea, over the birds of the air, and over the cattle, over all the earth and over every creeping thing that creeps on the earth." (Gen 1;26). God created us in the most beautiful image possible. We were made out of the wholeness of God and His Spirit. We tend to look at the sky and say things like, "look at God's masterpiece. He is such an artist." There is nothing wrong with this assessment of one aspect of God. I find it disturbing, however, that we don't look at ourselves in the mirror and marvel over God's creation in that same manner. When we see stripes of pink, blue and purple whisked across the sky, it sends us into a worship to the one who created it. Why can't we look at ourselves and flow into worship of our creator? Deception!

Please don't confuse what I just said with self-worship. It is being able to find the beauty in oneself knowing that our creator designed you intentionally with a purpose in mind. That is beautiful. It is for that reason that we give God praise. What we may look at and call a flaw, God thought of it, and saw a means whereby He could get glory from it. Praise God!

Adam and Eve were put out of the Garden. The beautiful place God created to commune with His beautiful creations. Why? Deception. The devil did not lie to Eve. The devil brought the truth into question. There is the root and momentum behind deception. Deception opens the door to disobedience. And that is what happened with Eve.

That is also what happened to me. January 31, 2016. Months leading up to this date, I had been succumbed by the spirit of depression. I fought so hard. But I fought alone. In 2015, my then, best friend and I, after rooming together for 4 years decided to get our own apartments. Actually, she decided to get one and I was sure that there was something more, the Lord had for me in Australia. Due to a pretty bad car accident a few days before I was scheduled to leave, where God literally spared my life, I was unable to fly. I actually returned to Chicago, not knowing the next steps for my life. Apparently, I had some more learning and growing to do in Kentucky. I stayed in Chicago for a few days and back to Kentucky I went. 2015 was one heck of a year. So many things happened that year that shaped my today. One of the biggest events was me coming into covenant relationship with my King, Jesus Christ. I gave Him the most wholehearted "YES" that year. Something came over me one night as I watched Pastor John on a Thursday night Bible study. The same pastor who had once been my youth pastor. God spoke through that man and I gave God my whole life that night.

Yet, a few months later I would find myself under the Spirit of heaviness. I thought there was something wrong with my, "Yes" to God. I thought it to be faulty. I became even more depressed. I started believing that I had once again lied to God. I had a rewards member card to the local smoke and spirit shop. I did not enter my home without at least two bottles of Sweet Red and enough juice for my modified "vape" machine.

I distinctly recall one day, it was some time in December of 2015, I touched the doorknob of my townhome and heard a voice that said, "Turn around you don't have any liquor." I was cold and tired. I had been at three of my four jobs that day. Yet, I turned around and went to go buy wine. The spirit of addiction spoke loud and clear and I responded. I felt so guilty. I was ashamed because I knew the covenant I had made with God.

Sometimes I cried out to God. Sometimes I did not. I didn't have my friend right there like she'd been all those years. Sometimes I felt suffocated. Like, I couldn't open my mouth. But tears would roll down the sides of my face as I would just think, "God I don't wanna live like this." Or "God I'm sorry" as I'd find myself refilling my glass. The devil had convinced me out of what I knew to be true. About who I was, who God is and what that meant for me and my identity. Not just in Christ. But simply, who I am. Too many times we've made that distinction. And although necessary in order to teach on Salvation, after Salvation your identity in Christ *is* your identity. This was part of my problem. I had an identity in Christ, and I had one that I did not allow anyone to see. This is how the enemy was able to keep me in depression for so long even after I'd gave God my BEST yes.

Here is the beauty. All that was happening to me, was not because I gave God another faulty, half-hearted, luke-warm, scrawny, little "Yes." It is because I indeed, gave God my most heart-filled, my most desperate, my most beautiful "Yes" that I could muster up after a year of being beat down. The enemy of my soul was literally SCARED out of his mind! All that had happened after that Thursday night Bible study, as I laid prostrate on my best friend's living room floor, committed to submit myself wholly unto God, was RIGHT! It was pure. And it was the thing that had long separated not only myself, but even members of my family from the future God promised us. There was nothing wrong with my YES. It was the perfect "Yes" that God could use.

Because of that, I came under attack. I did not know much about spiritual warfare, but I would soon learn. I'd begun attending a local church. It took much effort to make the decision to stop watching church online and join a local church. But I did. January 2016, we were on a corporate 21-day liquid-only fast. I was scared and excited because I had not done a 21-day liquid-only fast before. I thought I was going to die. I was still dealing with this depression and I had no one to talk to. I later found out that my best-friend at the time was going through her own spiritual battles. So, I'd come across this guy one night as I laid on my sofa, watching goofy sitcoms, drinking a bottle of wine and deciding whether or not to swipe left or right. I would use the social dating app, Tinder to past time as I would lay and watch TV. We both apparently "swiped right" and it was a match. I began texting and talking with this new guy pretty regularly over the course of a month's time.

I don't know how I got to this point. But I do recall, after eventually being obedient and breaking things off with Golden Man, feeling like no one would ever love me the way he did. Part of my attraction to him besides physically, was his ability to make me know how beautiful he believed I was. Not just in words. He marveled at my beauty as if it were his own beautiful masterpiece. And THAT is why, beauty is in *his* eye. In the eye of the FATHER. Father God (Abba), but also in the eye of the male. Oh Lord, please help the people that may be offended. I am here and so are you to literally obliterate the lies of hell with the truth of the Almighty God Himself. Beauty is in the eye of God because it is through that lens that we were created. We are made in His likeness, so our natural fathers have the ability to define for us how we receive love and perceive beauty.

To the surprise of some, women, as well as men, have been unintentionally wounded by natural fathers who may have failed to establish exactly what beauty is in their sons and daughters. These father wounds make it difficult for many to receive the truth that God created a beautiful creation, when He formed you and I. This also hinders many from fully receiving God as Father because we want to handle God, based on our interactions with our earthly Fathers. This is deception. And the only way to combat deception is by displacing it with God's truth.

"Your identity - the characteristics determining who you are as an individual - is that you are wholeheartedly loved by your Father God." -MLSIII

This new guy, let's call him 'Creed,' reminded me of the way I felt when I was with Golden Man. They both assured me, that I was beautiful. That is a powerful weapon. I had father figures throughout my life. Sadly, my own biological father wasn't there. He made a brief impact on my life a few times, but he was not consistent. God knew that, when He chose him as my father, and I believe with great conviction that He was very intentional in doing so. I received every good thing that my father had to offer, nothing more or less. Every good thing. God spared me of the parts of his life that might have spoiled the fruit, but chose the best seed my father had, he sowed it inside of my mother and produced a good thing. Does that not sound like the work of Abba? A good tree cannot bear bad fruit, nor *can* a bad tree bear good fruit (Matt 7:18).

Throughout my life, I have always had a yearning and desire to know God on a deeper level. Ever since I was a small child. The church that most of my family attends now, I actually went there first. I believe what led them there was my decision to become baptized at the age of five. I remember them all being there and becoming members shortly after.

Because my love for God has always been so strong, and God is not a man that He should lie, nor a son of man that He shall repent. Has He said, and will He not do?

Or has He spoken, and will He not make it good? (Num. 23:19). Then nothing, will separate my from His love. This is His promise. However, the Word accounts for the things that will *attempt* to come between God's love and us. For Adam and Eve it was nakedness (shame of sin). They believed that God looked at them differently after eating of the forbidden fruit. This distorted their view of our Father God. For me, it was darkness. Darkness distorted my view of the Father. But the Word of God assures us that we are conquerors of all things that may try to come between us and Father's love.

Romans 8:35-39 says:

"Who shall separate us from the love of Christ? Shall tribulation, or distress, or persecution, or famine, or nakedness, or peril, or sword? As it is written:

"For Your sake we are killed all day long;
We are accounted as sheep for the slaughter."
Yet in all these things we are more than conquerors
through Him who loved us. For I am persuaded that
neither death nor life, nor angels nor principalities nor
powers, nor things present nor things to come, nor
height nor depth, nor any other created thing, shall be
able to separate us from the love of God which is in
Christ Jesus our Lord." (KJV)

I could not see my Father and therefore I could not see myself. Since I could not see myself, I desired someone who would validate my beauty. Creed was excellent at that. We met up a few times before January. I had begun to learn about him and his children. We discussed his work and my work. I intentionally avoided the subject of faith.

At this point I was embarrassed, and I did not want to be a bad reflection of Christ. I was in sin, and I didn't want to be held accountable by my faith. That is as honest as anyone can possibly be when in sin. That is the place that allows conviction to do its job. It's that place of living a double life that makes conviction work so hard.

We dated. His birthday came around and he asked me to hang out with he and his friends in the city. I agreed. Before the start of the evening all of his friends bailed out on him. I lived thirty minutes outside of Louisville where we would be meeting. My Goddaughter had asked me to come over and watch a movie with her and I thought how beautiful, I now had an excuse to bail too, but I didn't bail.

I watched the movie with her, and she fell asleep. Her mother took her upstairs for bed and I thought she was going to return so we could have some girl talk. I really wanted to confess all that had been happening with me. But she yelled from upstairs, "Turn the lights off when you leave." I was already in a state of loneliness and depression, feeling rejected, I left to go get dressed to meet Creed.

That occurred on a Saturday night, January 30th, on his actual birthday. I had already purchased an outfit for the night and one for church the following Sunday morning. Sunday was consecration Sunday, the day we would end our fast with each other and in fellowship. I broke this fast once every week, at *least* during that fast. But that last week, I'd really been trying. I wanted to see something change in my life. Yet the night before church I met up with this guy for drinks.

Now there is no shame or guilt in this area for me at this time of my life, but I did feel shame and guilt as this all occurred. If you didn't know, that is not of God. God does not make you to feel ashamed of sin. He accounted for it. But God demonstrates His own love toward us, in that while we were still sinners, Christ died for us (Rom 5:8). The enemy likes to use shame and guilt as lock and key to keep us bound to sin. This is why we must know the truth. The aforementioned scripture literally means, before you or I were born, God planted His Son, Jesus Christ into the earth so that thousands of years before my or your birth, we'd be forgiven for the sins we were yet to commit.

One Stella and two glasses of Merlot. At 2:10a, the bartender said, "legally I can take that drink from you because it's after 2am and we are closed." Later after the rest of the events occurred, my best friend then, asked me "What does 2:10 mean to you?" I said that it was the time when the bartender made that comment. She said she woke up at that time and thought about me. She went back to sleep. I went on to the next bar with him. Two Car Bombs, two Heinekens and one shot of Jägermeister later, I found myself in the parking lot of the sports bar that we'd left, having sex in my car. Yep! I said I didn't want to be held to the standard of my faith, and MY GOD! I just dropped every standard I ever had. Six years of being abstinent, technically ended in that moment. However, I was abstaining but not necessarily living Holy.

The last guy that I had been with sexually was Golden man. And even after breaking up with him in 2011. We "re-visited" our situation in 2015 and although, sexual intercourse did not occur, we actually practiced something that I literally did not have language for. We made out (lots of kissing) but we practiced this breathing activity and through it, like we'd joined as one even without sexual penetration. Those same breathing and meditation practices were just another form of tantra. But God got me out of that jam, again.

As I look back over some of the types of situations that sin got me in, I see just how God has always kept His hand on me. This soul-tie took several sessions of deliverance to be released from and renunciations of false gods and deities channeled through these sexual practices. It also took much fasting. I went on a yearlong season of prayer and fasting to break free of the bondages of some strongholds like rejection, lust, addiction, and bitterness; which were only some of the sources behind this bastard-like behavior.

Today, one of the most powerful scriptures in my life,

"Flee sexual immorality. Every sin that a man does is outside the body, but he who commits sexual immorality sins against his own body. Or do you not know that your body is the temple of the Holy Spirit who is in you, whom you have from God, and you are not your own? For you were bought at a price; therefore glorify God in your body and in your spirit, which are God's" 1 Cor. 6:18-20. (NKJV)

"Whom you have from God," means who is given to you from God. We are not our own in the body of Christ. There are rules and standards and such. The same way you knew not to sit on great-grandma's living room furniture if you grew up in a black household prior to the 1980's. Or how you knew not to play outside in your school clothes. They reminded us often as to why you could not do what you wanted to do in your school clothes or in their living room, it's because "you didn't pay for it." The word of God reminds us that we were bought with a price. Therefore, we ought to be mindful to honor God in our bodies as well. However, I had distanced myself from this truth in that moment.

As I drove home, tired and intoxicated, I tried keeping my eyes open and I was barely doing a decent job at it when I pulled off to the rest stop near my exit. I actually thought it was my exit. I parked and figured I'd go to sleep, but even in this drunken stupor, I noticed a truck driver that made me feel very uncomfortable. My stop was the next exit, so I decided to go for it. As I came off of the ramp, I must have dozed off.

When I opened my eyes, I saw the red light and tried hitting the brakes, but it was too late, I coasted right across the intersection. It was 5:23 am in a small town, the roads were clear thank God, but parked right behind me were the police. I went to jail immediately! I had never been in any trouble with the law before. I was scared out of my mind. I became sober very quickly, or so I thought. I'll say I became very alert.

I got booked. I sat in that jail cell for thirteen hours. I literally call that moment my "Saul to Paul." I felt like God knocked me off the path of destruction and blinded me with His glory.

For thirteen straight hours of my life, as my natural inclination was to panic and worry, God wrapped His arms around me so tightly. For thirteen hours my Father, who had been here for my entire life, witnessed all of my mess-ups, stood there when I ignored Him, acted like I never knew him sometimes in my actions, this beautiful man, my Daddy, held me in His arms for thirteen hours. I cried. I cried. I cried. I apologized. I apologized. I apologized. I was forgiven. He held me tighter. He comforted me. He did not judge me. He loved on me. I confessed my every sin. I mean every single one. I declared that I would not do those things again. I told Him that my only desire for my new life would be to please Him. And He said, "I know". I received that in my heart. Keep in mind, I had a lot of gunk around my heart, but with everything I had, I held on to knowing how assured He was in my desire to live a life pleasing in His sight. His surety spoke to my genetic makeup.

My DNA heard its creator and began to realign itself to its original state. In that moment I opened my eyes and I saw my Daddy. He was so beautiful. His beauty assured me of my very own beauty. In that moment, God held the very definition of who I was, in His eyes.

Mirror Mirror on The Wall:
Time to Reflect

Take a moment to either, find one, or go to a mirror and look at yourself. If you do not have the physical capability of sight, get to a quiet space and allow God to give you images of who you are.

If you think of yourself as one way that does not agree with the word of God, allow Him to give you a new image.

For example, if people have called you ugly or stupid, allow God to give you a new image. And meditate on that image until it reaches your heart. You will know when it reaches your heart because it will feel as though someone has taken a dirty glass window and used the best glass cleaner on the market to clean it.

This exercise is to allow God the opportunity to "Clean up" your vision of yourself.

Chapter 3
You're so Beautiful... to be Dark-Skinned!

"TURTLE SUNDAE"

About a year ago, I was at this dope annual event in Hyde Park, Chicago hosted by The Silver Room. I ran into my cousin, who then ran into one of our mutual childhood friends. Actually, the two of them were friends first. I moved into the area and transferred to their school and it was almost an instant fit for the three of us.

Remember, in the very beginning of this book I talked about how our community in Florida was predominantly white? Well, oddly enough, white people weren't the first group of people to make me aware of race and skin color? Yeah! My first lessons about racism actually came from within the African American community.

I have dark skin. I love my complexion but that hasn't always been the case. As a matter of fact, it was an entry way for self-hatred and jealousy to creep into my heart by way of comparison. When the old crew and I linked up at this event, not having been in the same place all at once in almost 20 years, one of the first comments that were made was about complexion.

See, my cousin is very fair-skinned, back in the day she would have been called a red-bone. Wait is that Midwest slang? I don't know, but if it is, now you know something new. Our mutual friend has a golden complexion. Her name literally means gold in Spanish. She has a caramel complexion. Then there is me, touched, kissed and just loved on by the sun. I have heard the saying, "The blacker the berry, the sweeter the juice," probably way too many times to count, surely, before I had formed a context around what that statement even meant.

My caramel friend says, at our impromptu meet-up, "I was just telling a friend the other day that I am the caramel one (in defense of not being the dark one), there was a dark-skinned and a light-skinned one in our little group! Like vanilla, caramel and chocolate!" On this day, that comment didn't bother me. Actually, she was just recalling the way we were labeled back then. Whenever someone referred to one of us but didn't know the name they resorted to complexion. For example, "I can't think of her name but the dark-skinned girl who's always with the light-skinned girls." It would happen to them too in that same way.

The thing that bothered me then, was that it was simply "a thing." When trying to describe anyone the first description was that of their complexion. Which meant, when the stories came back, I heard a lot of "Where's the cute dark-skinned girl"? My friend's family were from another state when they would visit, they were looking for the dark one.

Being the dark one, or the dark-skinned one wouldn't have seemed so bad if it weren't for a saying that made me question everything dark for most of my life; "You're so pretty... to be dark-skinned."

I just wanted to snatch the ellipsis right out of midair and hurl them into the Dead Sea, because that's how I wanted them... dead. Who would have known that three small periods could take a girl's esteem from all the way up here (imagine the very top of your favorite rollercoaster), to all the way down here (imagine your ice cream hitting the ground on a Nevada Summer's day)! In one breath they would pay a compliment and snatch it back like a yo-yo. I never understood why, you're so beautiful needed that caveat, or did it?

Well, the truth is, it did because it was to make me feel as though I was the exception. I've actually spoken to people who have given this God-awful compliment and they really do not mean it in a negative way. In their defense they meant in the highest regard possible. Well then, my next question becomes, "Why?" Here's the thing, in American culture, sorry folks we have to go here for a moment, after a time where folks were settled in their original lands but before now there was a stint of some 400+ years of slavery. Stay with me now, this is history and history help mold a people. I mean we are still living by a document (U.S. Constitution) that was written over 200+ years ago so let's not pick and choose what history we want to accept.

Anyway, back to slavery in America. Africans, now African Americans, after losing their identity, began to grab onto any form of identity they could. Slave masters for their own reasons and means of control, would pick some slaves to remain in their homes, these were often who they deemed pretty, mainly fair-skinned.

Unfortunately, most of them were abused in a sexual manner. Among the other slaves it may have looked as though they received preferential treatment by the slave master. I'm sure the house slaves would just as rather be free than to have to endure any of it at all. But it drew a division among the African slaves, who had already lost their identity, trying to find a new identity in this new place. Except what was being taught is that, you're only good for the work of the field and if you're pretty enough you might be good for your looks and body.

It doesn't take many, if any words to convey such a strong message like that to a vulnerable people. After slavery, there were Jim Crow laws. The lighter folk tried passing for white, because white people were the chosen, right? They had all of the power. Who wouldn't want power? Heck, who wouldn't just want food? I mean white people could walk into any diner, white or black and be welcomed. But being black meant you were restricted to black only business or run-down places with no accommodations. We couldn't swim in swimming pools with white people. Now, to a people with no identity, or fractured identity, it is sad but natural to want to claim the one with the best benefits.

This is my personal observation, love of research, history and study of African Americans, politics and governmental issues in this country as it relates to socio-economic matters. Others may not agree with the conclusion that I've come up with that says, self-hatred among African Americans is a demon that was given access when a people were stripped of everything, they once thought of themselves and told it was wrong.

So, light-skinned is better than dark-skinned. Somewhere between then and even now, this is the conclusion that was drawn. So I spent most of my life trying to figure out why I couldn't just be pretty. Why did it have to have that caveat on the end?

I thought this just caused self- esteem issues. I figured I would put everyone's attention on everything else about me so that they wouldn't focus on my skin. For example, I wore really strange clothes, we talked about this. Actually, I wore very nice clothes, but I would do strange things to them. I would distress my denim before it became popular. I wore my jeans inside out! I would wear the same style shoe but in different colors (one black shoe and one white shoe). I would do all types of things to my hair; I mean crazy stuff. Ohhh, and don't forget the gray contact lenses, they were my

American Express, I never left home without those. As a teen I remember questioning God about why He would make some people light-skinned and some dark-skinned. I often wondered what I would look like with light skin. I was never brave, or I guess, desperate enough to try bleaching or go to any of those lengths. But I was definitely curious. I don't have the time or expertise to dive into this topic, but skin bleaching is definitely a culture and one worth examining. Many people are feeling hurt and abandoned and are not even sure why. We have to share God's love. It is important that we work on ourselves so that we can be a help to others.

I didn't realize that this not only caused insecurities and low self-esteem; but this was another form of rejection and self-hatred all of which had to be dealt with during deliverance. But most importantly, it had to be displaced by me receiving God's love.

Mirror Mirror on The Wall:
Time to Reflect

In this reflection, I want you to use this writing prompt and write until you have nothing else to say.

"[Insert your name here], you're simply beautiful because:" Here is where you will list every beautiful thing about yourself. List scriptures that God has used to encourage you, encouraging words from your friends and family, physical attributes of beauty, etc. Before the end of this book my prayer is that, we bust out of deception by declaring truth over ourselves and into our lives.

It is my prayer in this exercise specifically, that we learn that our own beauty does not take anything away from our sisters or brothers in Christ. But that our collective beauty enhances the Kingdom of God.

Chapter 4
For real...Do I look like a Boy?

"THE BIG CHOP...AGAIN...AND AGAIN!"

Recently I cut my hair. "Big Chop" he yelled as he grabbed a bundle of my locs with a pair of gigantic scissors. This was indeed a big chop. However, I had never felt readier to rid myself of this weight. My locs were beautiful. Outside of the first six months I did them myself. And even during those first six months my best friend at the time who started them, was the only one who I allowed to handle them. They were in fact my babies. And this big chop was in fact, not the first.

I feel like I have experienced many "Big Chops" throughout my life. I am recalling a time when I had to be about six or seven years old. My father, a well-known gangster in the city of Chicago, had me out with him for the day. I don't have many memories of he and I in this way. I feel like I experienced so many crazy things in this one day because I don't recall ever hanging out with him alone any other time. Yet, I recall shopping for bomber jackets for myself and my little brother, who was with us for a portion of the day. We got pizza that day as well. I also recall being in this store. I know exactly where the store was, that big abandoned store in 5th City, on Chicago's Westside. They started shooting while we were in that store. I was scared to tears. But strangely I remember feeling safe with my father being next to me. He wasn't crouched down beside me, he stood, next to me after he put me down near a rack of chips. He stood there as if nothing, would touch me or him. Before now, I couldn't recall a time as a young child when my father made me feel safe. I grew up at first, not even knowing that my biological was my father.

My mother married a man who was headed for the U.S Air Force right after high school. This is the man I knew as my father. Darnell, now passed away, was the love of my life. I was his princess. His baby girl. I could do no wrong in his sight. There wasn't anything that I couldn't ask for or do. And maybe there were things that he said no to, but I don't remember them. I don't ever remember a time when I felt disappointed by him. Well, there is the one time...his death.

There was a day that we took photos all day long. We lived in Tampa, Fl. And we had this nice fountain in the courtyard of our condo. He and I took pictures out there all day. This man made me feel safe always! He would hold me in his arms, and I felt like I could and would do everything in life that I wanted to do. At that time, I just wanted to live in a castle and marry a handsome prince. I wanted to have five children. I used to love fairytales and princesses before Disney made them a cash cow, Cinderella, Belle and Ariel were the pinnacle of my aspirations.

Let me make this clear, I didn't want to *be* them, I already felt like I was among them, as princesses. My daddy made me feel like royalty. And therefore, I believed that if those princesses got the big house with the handsome prince, then so would I.

This is the formation of our identity, of our beauty, begins… in the eyes of our father.

"For you did not receive the spirit of bondage again to fear, but you received the Spirit of adoption by whom we cry out, "Abba, Father." The Spirit Himself bears witness with our spirit that we are children of God,"
Romans 8:15-16(NKJV)

In my daddy's arms I was assured of my identity! I am safe it said. I am protected it said. I am loved it said. I am strong it said. I am courageous it said. I am royalty it said. I lack nothing it said. I AM BEAUTIFUL IT SAID.

One day, it all went away! He died in a car accident when I was about five years old. I lost the father I'd known my entire life, and in some ways, I lost my mother as well. Things got really difficult for my mother and I during this time. Things that appeared one way, was actually another and nothing seemed stable or safe. I found myself being more comfortable with my own little fairy tales. A place where I would go to escape the uncertainty of my new life. I began wanting everything that I did not have. Instead of feeling like I was a princess I felt like I had been thrown into the dungeon, in rags. I felt abandoned, and with abandonment comes rejection; and rejected people reject people, ideas and most detrimentally, they reject *truth!*

All of those things that I had believed this man, my daddy, told me and assured me of felt like a lie because he left my life. As a child I could not fathom his purpose in my life as a way of establishing a necessary identity so that as I grew older, I would be secure as a daughter. Instead I believed the opposite. The opposite of truth… I was waddling in deception at the age of five years old and there was no one there with truth in their mouth to reel me back in.

Fast forward back to Chicago two years later, and I'm spending the day with my biological father. He only has this one daughter, whom he hasn't had to take care of ever, so hair is an issue. He takes me to this beauty salon on the corner of Chicago Ave and Homan, where my mother would later become a stylist, to get my hair done.

As aforementioned, my father was a well-known gangster and drug dealer, people saw money when they saw him. He took me into this beauty shop to get my hair done. Understand, this was no scene from Poetic Justice when Janet's character put all of those beautiful ponytails and bows in Lucky's daughter's hair. No! This beautician saw dollar signs when she saw my father and she gave me the most expensive hairstyle on the list…The Jheri Curl. My dad did not know what she was going to do. He said to the stylist, "Do whatever you want, I don't know," and he left. When he came back, I had a Jheri Curl. My mother had a fit. I remember her telling me this story and she said, "I was livid! Why would he allow them to put a curl in your hair?!"

I went to school in the late eighties early nineties looking like a member of Run DMC or one of the Cold Crush Brothers! I love hip-hop. Anyway, this was the first time that I noticed myself not comparing myself to the standard of beauty associated with princesses and royalty, but rather with the brute or rather ugliness of a man. No, I am not bashing men and I think men are some of God's most beautiful creatures. But in this instance, I no longer associated my appearance as a little girl with other girls, I, with this short hair and activator dripping down the sides of my face, felt as though I resembled a boy.

I remember one day after I'd gotten this Jheri curl, my mother and I were rushing off to school and work. Part of the Jheri Curl process included wearing a plastic shower cap on your head as you slept to keep the curls moisturized. This particular morning, I ran into my classroom late and everyone was staring at me. I couldn't understand why until my teacher pointed it out to me that I had a cap on my head. These children some black some white, mostly white, couldn't understand why I had this on my head. I was so embarrassed. I didn't want to be in that room. I wanted to close my eyes and disappear as I often times did. I would close my eyes and take myself to other places where I was beautiful, loved and extremely happy. I believe this is when I became aware of something called, "Escapism." Society calls it daydreaming.

After that I went home and cried. I cried a lot as a child. I was called cry baby often. I told my mother I didn't want a Jheri curl anymore because I was too embarrassed. Now, for those who *really* have no idea of what a Jheri Curl is, it is a chemical process of turning coarse hair into these huge (loose) curls using a chemical solution. You rod the hair and use this other chemical to set the curls. It's a whole thing. But it's not easily reversed. The only way to really come out of the Jheri curl style was to cut it off. My mother did not want to do that, so she tried stripping the chemicals out and I don't think that worked because I recall my very first "Big Chop" the summer before 2nd grade.

I had a mini afro. But my mom was the bomb. I started wearing braids and this became a part of my identity. Sort of like the singer Brandy. We all knew her for her braids, and actually I felt that I now had a girl who was beautiful, and I could identify with her. She became my favorite artist. I now had an identity to latch on to that allowed me to feel beautiful and confident in who I was. But that wasn't my own identity I was just becoming comfortable with someone else's.

I wore braids until I was in 7th grade. That is when I transferred to the school on the near West-Side. This was a time when I was determined to establish my own identity. This is when I decided that, "Hey! The best person to try to be like was myself!" And that's exactly what I did, or so I thought.

Over those years my hair had grown tremendously and now that I was out of braids, I wanted to show my creativity through my hairstyles. By this time my mother worked at the very salon where my father had taken me as a little girl. I'd worn so many different styles over the years. In 2004, my mom got remarried and I cut my hair the shortest it had ever been. However, it was straightened with a relaxer and very well received by my family and friends. Everyone spoke of how beautiful it was and how mature I looked, I was approaching twenty so that was a huge compliment.

However, only 2 short years later I made the decision to "go natural" no perm and no one in my family to give me pointers. At the time I lived in Hyde Park. I loved living in this area there was so many beautiful black people. The many shops and restaurants that made me feel like this is the place for me. Hyde Park had its own style and still does. It gave me this sense of liberation that I had never felt before. I, confidently, walked into Yehia's, ready for this "Big Chop" they called out in the shop. Although I had been in this place before, cutting my hair completely off. I had not been in this place in my life before, confident about who I was and how the world perceived me to be. For the first time I'd felt as though those two views matched up. That is, until the woman turned me around to look at myself in the mirror. I smiled but inside I SCREAMED. It was like the summer before 2nd grade all over again. I looked at myself and recalled Clarence from Coming to America saying, "Dang Boy! What's this some type of weave or something"! I straight up felt and looked like Eddie Murphy in that movie. My hair was natural with multiple textures, but the front had this little lip of hair over my forehead and I about lost it.

My best friend and I walked back to our apartment. I went in my room and cried. One thing you'll notice that comes along with the spirit of rejection is hypersensitivity. Everything made me cry. Most times it would keep me from functioning. Especially if I were alone. Most times if I had someone around who could talk me through this, I wouldn't stay there. Again, I cannot stress enough how beautiful deliverance is, it is an inheritance to us as Children of God.

Once I finished crying, I went into my bathroom and looked at myself like "GOD REALLY?! DO I LOOK LIKE A BOY?!" I realized right there that in fact, my outward identity was not the same as my inward identity and that what I had allowed people to perceive me as was actually a façade. I walked around as this confident woman. Bold and fearless, but when I looked at myself in the mirror, I did not see fearlessness, I saw shame and insecurity. I did not see any of the beauty I had allowed others to believe I believed about myself.

In this life, there has to be a spiritual BIG CHOP and sometimes one is not enough. We go through the processes of deliverance and we believe that we are free and clear of the demons that have tormented us and kept us caged most of our lives. When the truth is, they've grown with us so closely that sometimes they blend in with our personality. What does this mean? It means we still have work to do. It means that you could very well need to experience another BIG CHOP before we actually get down to the root of the problem.

I believe my first Big Chop at the age of seven was the biggest. It exposed that big Ole' demon of self-hatred and insecurity. It exposes the spirits of comparison and competition, and even years later when I thought I'd grown up and gotten through all of those things, my second Big Chop revealed, nope they were not gone just hidden.

Thankfully, I had a friend at the time because as she laughed at the fact that I kept doing these Coming to America lines, she walked across the street with me to Walgreens for a solution to remedy my problem. We came back with a Dark & Lovely hair bleaching kit and a pair of scissors. We clipped that lip off the front of my hair, added some color and it became one of my best looks to date.

Again, I didn't deal with the actual issues. Which brings me to my most recent BIG CHOP! October 1, 2011, I started to loc my hair. Although, the commitment to do so, came many months prior. One afternoon as I looked at myself in the mirror playing with my hair. My mother was a beautician, I did not fear styling, coloring, or perming my hair on my own. I'd recently shaved one side of my hair off because this was during the time when Cassie, the singer, was wearing one side long and the other side shaven. Yup! I jumped the bandwagon. I had been wearing a Mohawk for a while anyway, I didn't feel uneasy about this style.

Anyway, I'm styling the large portion of hair and as I held it in my hand it was very drastic from one extreme to the other. God began to speak to me in that moment about how this was reflective of the life I had been living. He used my half shaved, half grown out hair style to minister to my life. I am often tickled that God knows the exact measures to take to speak to His babies. Anyone else could have been doing the same exact thing and not received this message. Take heart in knowing that God in heaven knows YOU! He knows your every thought and created you oh so wonderfully.

"O Lord, You have searched me and known me"
Ps. 139:1(NKJV)

God knew just how to reach the depths of my soul. He said to me, "Choose ye this day." I will be honest, I didn't know what that meant. But the Lord kept speaking to me. He said, far too long you've been all in and jumped out, all in and then jumped out. No, beautiful people, he was not talking about a game of double-dutch, he was talking about my relationship with Him. Before this moment I would have moments in my life where I was on FIRE for Christ. And then something, or someone, (I had a weakness for the male species to be specific) would come and I would stumble and fall off course. Relationships were actually my weakness and the devil knew it. Just when I would be on fire for the Lord, feeling as though nothing could bring me down. I would in fact, come under this attack of loneliness. Then, I would get a slew of action, seemingly out of nowhere. New baes, foreign baes, fine baes, old baes shoot I have a picture or two floating around there with some "who done it and what for" baes. Ex baes were the worst. Because the Lord knows His children, He will help us out of a thing that we would not otherwise come out of.

I remember a relationship in particular with this guy, I pause here because as I began to write the storyline I had at least two guys pop into my mind. Which means it was not the guy at all but there was a cycle. A pattern if you will, that was attractive to me. There were these guys, both beautiful men, well one was gorgeous, we talked about him in "Golden Man". The other was beautiful because I wanted him to be. He is who I called "Superman".

"Superman" was a praise and worship leader and the other was, Golden Man. "Superman" was a former drug addict, I didn't know this prior to us dating. However, I was trying something new. I actually thought He was sent from God. He embodied a lot of the things I had prayed and asked God to send me in a mate. Because I had this thought, there were a lot of things I ignored about his character. He was a liar. He mismanaged money. He was all out shady, and I looked past all of that because I was like hey, maybe I'm supposed to be a light to him, right? Wrong! God won't send you a mate who takes you away from Him or the purpose He has for your life. I had started back smoking weed, skipping work and fornicating while being involved with this man. Uh, DING! DING! DING! that wasn't God! One day while trying to leave for work, this man drove his old school Lincoln Town Car behind my car, blocked me in and told me I wasn't going anywhere. I was on the phone with my best friend at the time, who was still living in Chicago, and she was like "Do I need to send my cousins over there?"

Let me take a minute to encourage you, that even your most saved friends must not be afraid to throw hands or at *least* have "people." Hear me?! He backed up and got out of my way, because if you remember, I hadn't had my "Saul to Paul" just yet. I was quick to get all the way out of character with whoever wanted it. However, all the crazy didn't belong to him. I own my portion as well. I began backing my car up praying he moved his before I did too much damage. As I drove off I thanked God for showing me who he was but also showing me who I was. I was very damaged. But God saw fit to preserve me.

Back to the man… well… woman in the mirror. These experiences had flooded my mind when I heard the Lord say, "Choose ye this day". But I had no clue as to what that looked like. In that small voice, my sins were exposed, my shame and guilt had to take a back seat because they were lies that had been confronted by the truth. Like the woman at the well. God had just aired out all of my messy, dirty laundry to me, as if I wasn't aware. He did so in a way that let me know that He was aware. But that He still had a place in His heart for me.

"Now therefore, fear the Lord, serve Him in sincerity and in truth, and put away the gods which your fathers served on the other side of the River and in Egypt. Serve the Lord! And if it seems evil to you to serve the Lord, choose for yourselves this day whom you will serve, whether the gods which your fathers served that were on the other side of the River, or the gods of the Amorites, in whose land you dwell. But as for me and my house, we will serve the Lord"
Josh 24:14-15 (NKJV)

In the mirror that day I committed my whole heart to God. Now, to be clear, it was not some instant turnaround. I believe this was the first step in the right direction. It was, however, a change of heart. It was the beginning of a transformation. I went ahead and got the rest of my hair cut off. I don't call this a big chop because most of my hair was already cut. But now so was my heart. I had begun to allow God to circumcise my heart.

As my hair grew out, I'd already made the decision to loc my hair. As I mentioned earlier in this story, I was natural before. I would not loc, because I used to say, "Y'all know I have commitment issues" when people would ask me about growing locs. When I chose the Lord that day in the mirror, I decided to loc my hair that day also. I decided to allow God to have my heart. Still not knowing what that meant. I didn't really realize that it was the beginning of a beautiful process.

October 1, 2011, I had enough hair to twist and the external loc'ing process began. I had made the internal decree and now was the part when others were able to witness. My Apostle often says, every seed starts out in darkness. And the seed of my commitment had started out in my heart in a private place between myself and the Lord and now it was the time where my declaration was budding out for the world to see. I had experienced so many trials during this phase. I was used to being able to wash my hair daily. Now I could not wash it at all. In this process of renewal, I felt dirty. Then when I was able to wash my hair, I had to wear this stocking cap on my little buds so not to disturb the buds. Had I washed them without this cap to keep them in place, I would have ruined the progress.

I went through seasons of comparison as my locs grew at their very own rate. I had to change the products I used as they grew because what was good for the babies were not good for the adolescent. If you know locs, this is how the stages are described.

My first decision to loc my hair was in 2011. This was also a reflection of my spiritual journey and relationship with Christ. I didn't have the moment where I was desperate enough to change my ways until 2015. I didn't have my "Saul to Paul" until January 2016. I am saying this to say, our journeys towards Christ cannot be compared to one another. In God's timing the Bible says, everything is made beautiful. I believe as the word continues, that God hides us, most times from ourselves. We wouldn't know what to do with everything all at once that God has prepared for us.

The 5 stages to loc your hair is similar to a human cycle of maturation. Babies, Buds, Adolescents, Mature and Beyond Mature. It's been two years since I cut my hair. "Big Chop" he yelled as he grabbed a bundle of my locs with a pair of gigantic scissors. This was indeed a big chop. The date was September 30, 2017, 364 days before it would be my 6th year of having locs. God spoke to me days leading up to this Big Chop. I knew I was supposed to do it a day before it would make six years. He said, "The difference a day makes." That wasn't the first time I'd heard this from God. When I heard God at the end of 2016 instructing me to return to live in Chicago and to join my now church, All Nations Worship Assembly – Chicago (HQ), the very first series of the year was entitled, "Training Day: The Difference A Day Makes"

See in the 5th stage of having locs, the "Beyond Mature" stage looks different depending on the condition of your locs up until this point. Mine were pretty healthy and had grown very long. But for many people this is the stage where locs start growing thin and some begin to fall out. When God started revealing to me that I would cut my locs and exactly when I would do it, I started to understand why. The weight of my locs at their length now had the potential to begin destroying something that He intended to be beautiful. I had carried these locs and the lessons of my journey to its "Beyond Mature" stage. This stage can be detrimental in our spiritual journey. That is why following the voice of God and being obedient is very important.

In these last two years I had begun to pray for the knowing of God's divine timing. To move when God says move. To go when God says "Go". To stay when God says "stay." This was not only symbolic of God granting me that anointed but also, God revealing His plans for my future. And the things of the past could not go. In many ways, my last "Big Chop" was me shedding my old experiences, not negating the lessons learned (growth), but embracing the "new" place that God was taking me. And the way that this works is by growing through each stage, each journey, each lesson and becoming greater because of it. Rather than becoming stuck there.

Mirror Mirror on The Wall:
Time to Reflect

What has God *clearly* told you to "BIG CHOP" out of your life? I want to emphasize, what has *God* told you to cut out of your life? I warn you, please obey. Do not carry things of past into your future. You may not arrive at the future God planned for you if you do.

And Samuel said to Saul, "You have done foolishly. You have not kept the commandment of the Lord your God, which He commanded you. For now the Lord *would have* established your kingdom over Israel forever. Samuel 13:13 (emphasis made by me).

Chapter 5
Beauty and the Beast

"NELLA"

In "Turn the Tide", I briefly mentioned my childhood boyfriend and how this relationship would later become an ungodly soul tie that took great effort to come out of agreement with. As a young girl trying to protect my image of innocence, I gave my boyfriend the alias "Nella." This was that double life that I would continue to live, even throughout adulthood. I thought Nella sounded like a girl's name. I gave him a feminine alias so that I could cover up our relationship. My mother was ok with me having female friends. She was actually ok with my male friends but only those, that never posed the threat of boyfriend material. Anyway, he was Nella on the phone and in the little notes we'd write, I never actually thought about what it might imply if my mother had found those notes lol. Because he wasn't shy at all. Actually, for an 11-year old, he was quite in-tune with his feelings and emotions. He was very bold and forthcoming with his feelings about me.

Up until this point, I had had two boyfriends and a ton and a half of crushes. I was a dreamer and I lived often in fantasyland, which I addressed in "The Big Chop... Again...And Again". This was a breeding ground for depression in later years of my life. I'd created this place to escape reality. I lived there often. I learned that I had control over my thoughts. I also learned that my thoughts were powerful. As I think back on this story and others like it, I wonder if that is why I experienced many attacks on my mind throughout life.

I was aware of the power behind thought, the word of God says,

"For as he thinks in his heart, so is he"
Pr. 23:7a (NKJV)

I believe the enemy knew that I was aware of that power and began devising a plan of attack.

Back to Nella. He did not go to my school which was odd for me, I was a bit of a stalker back in the day. It wasn't intentional, but I am definitely a face to face communicator. I like the closeness of those types of interactions. I enjoy not only hearing one communicate with me but also watching people communicate, non-verbally as well. The two previous boyfriends that I'd had were both students in my old schools. We were always in the same classroom as well, speaking of my previous boyfriends.

Out the gate, Nella was different. He was this "big headed Lil boy", as every uncle, brother or mother in the hood has called the unsuspecting guy who dates their daughter, niece or sister. He had these huge lips. And the most brilliant smile. I remember thinking I've never seen anyone with a smile brighter than my own. I would compare him to Morris Chestnut, the Morris from "The Brothers" not the "Boyz in The Hood" Morris. Anyway, I am really jumping ahead of myself here. Because initially I didn't like him at ALL! I had actually told him "no" twice before when he asked me to go out with him.

But one day all of that changed. I like to say that he trapped me in an elevator. He would probably say that he was acting on a prime opportunity. Carpe Diem at its finest. One day, while at the Boys and Girls Club, Nella stopped me on the first floor by the elevator and asked me AGAIN, if I'd be his girlfriend. I had turned him down several times before, but he was quite persistent.

To be honest, all of that Morris Chestnut good looking black man stuff came much later, initially I was not attracted to him. I had always had a "type" in kind of how "the one" would look. And he wasn't it. I told you all that I lived in fantasyland. Since I was about 6 years-old I had always imagined what my Prince Charming would look like and the exact details of our wedding. We would have five children, they would all be athletic; and become these famous track, basketball and golf phenome. I didn't see that in him.

This day there was an added element to his proposal. As I stood and waited on the elevator, he asked me if I would be his girlfriend. Instead of the "no" I had previously given him, I gave him more of a shrug. And there was his glimmer of hope.

Not to, in any way, compare the man "Nella" to the enemy but I would like to pause here to point out exactly what the enemy looks like when he is in pursuant of you. In law enforcement there's something called an act "in furtherance." A young lady at my church preached a five-minute sermonette on the topic. She said being in law enforcement, if a person walked up to her and said they were going to commit a crime, she would have no legal right to arrest them without an act "in furtherance." But with that confession, she would then continue surveillance on that person, waiting and watching for that act. She then said, that's how the enemy watches our confessions to Christ. Sitting back waiting for you to commit an act "in furtherance" and the moment you do not, that's his point of entry.

This elevator moment was a clear depiction of why John writes,

So then, because you are lukewarm, and neither cold nor hot,[a] I will vomit you out of My mouth
Rev. 3:16 (KJV)

I had not given him a yes or a no and therefore, left a door of opportunity open. The enemy waits patiently for moments   like   this   in   our   lives.

Not only did I leave a spiritual door open for Nella, I also left a physical one open as well. He seized the opportunity at hand and joined me on my very brief elevator ride. There were only two levels in the Boys and Girls Club, we were on level one, but a lot happened in this short ride.

He slid onto the elevator with me, with hope in his eyes and an obscene amount of confidence in his heart. He asked me one more time, "will you go with me?" This time literally backing me into a corner, his big eyes and long eyelashes, now very low and persuasive. He grabbed the palms of my hands with his thumbs and very gently messaged them. I remember my little heart was about to beat out of my chest. I knew he was going in for the kill, I mean kiss.

My own logic was completely shot at this point. Emotion and flesh. Flesh and emotion. Those were the driving forces, oh and hormones, that made this moment what it was never supposed to be. He took one hand away from mine and held my chin between his index finger and his thumb. His very large lips came close to mine and his breath smelled of Flamin' Hot Cheetos!!! This was the last thing I remember before we were in a full-on lip locking session.

By the end of this, I cannot express enough, very short elevator ride I had become Mrs. "Nella." I recall tasting this stickiness that I attribute to the chemically packed bag of Flamin' Hots that he'd eaten right before kissing me. That taste lasted in my mouth way too long actually. Even as it slowly went away, I never forgot that taste, that smell, that moment where I threw everything that I had promised God out the door.

I recall telling God up until this point that my first kiss would happen the day of my wedding. I truly desired to do things pleasing in the sight of God. How did I know what was pleasing and what wasn't? I had enough examples of what was not, in my life. People in my family who would say, "I know God" they would then say, "Do as I say, not as I do." That last one was the dead giveaway that something wasn't right. Why was I to do as you said with your words, and not model the behaviors of your actions? I was a child, but I was an extremely intelligent child and with those words I formed my own way of living according to the Bible. Unfortunately, I had fallen prey at an early age, twelve, to the same enemy that had been after the other teenage   women   in   my   family.

Make no mistake about it, the devil intended to keep me bound to this man for a lifetime. Causing me to live outside of the will of God. Some may be thinking at this point, "it was just an innocent kiss", "puppy love is normal" or "teenage love is so cute and innocent". But I would emphatically disagree. It is indeed not innocent at all. In fact, the Bible warns us, "...do not awaken love until the time is right" (Song of Songs 2:7).

This one kiss alone unlocked emotions that I did not know existed inside of me. It brought fantasies about, that were unhealthy. It was not only a distraction, as I constantly doodled our names everywhere and onto everything I owned, but it also gave my mothers and grandmothers demons access to my life now. My mother was a teenage mother. She actually did not like my father very much at all. She says, "he was not cute to me at all!" I found myself thinking once, "well dang! What do you feel about me?" If you see a picture of the two of us together, his face is the male version of mine. It is quite scary actually. But she went ahead and dated him anyway. Here she is "going out" with a guy she didn't even like. However, emotions get involved and it changes the nature of your thoughts. Here I was "going out" with a guy that I didn't even like. However, emotions got involved and it changed the nature of my thoughts. A coincidence? No, not at all. I mentioned earlier that the devil is patient! How patient? He is patient throughout generations.

I can't be held accountable for my mother's sins. The devil is a legalist he is very aware of this.

Yet say you, why? does not the son bear the iniquity of the father? When the son has done that which is lawful and right, and has kept all my statutes, and has done them, he shall surely live Eze. 18:19 (KJ2000B).

According to scripture God doesn't desire to punish us for our parent's sin as long as we keep to His law and walk upright before Him, we are promised an abundant life with Christ. However, sins of a family can give the enemy access to future generations. And if the enemy can get you to commit the same sin as your family line, he can trick you into believing in some demons as "heredity" and that you have no control over it. Continuous cycles of generational curses. I very distinctly recall a family member once telling me, "you're going to be just like your mother, sixteen and pregnant." I had vowed not to ever be like my mother. I didn't want to be a teenage mother. But here I was locking lips and swapping spit in an elevator with a guy that I didn't even like, at the age of twelve. So yeah, some thought our relationship was cute and innocent even. But the devil, he had been watching for that act of "in furtherance" and here was, what he thought, his golden ticket.

I recall this time of my life feeling like the best and worst times of my early teenage years. There was this rush that I would get being with Nella. But I felt torn between right and wrong, good and evil and I did not like the feeling at all. I would be able to hide from people, but I knew God was always watching. I lived most of these years in guilt and shame.

This relationship not only stirred up love before it's time, it stirred up lust, perversion and a lying tongue. Yeah, the devil wanted me very badly. Well, he wanted my future. You've heard me emphasize this throughout the book because it is that serious. To the devil, you are barely a name on a page. It is with heaven's endorsement that you become more. The bigger the threat you pose to the kingdom of darkness the bigger the plot you become on his radar.

I would watch romantic movies and fantasize at night. I thought of how my wedding would be, how we would consummate the wedding on our wedding night and then how I would become pregnant almost instantly. All of this seemed ok to me. I wasn't in sexual sin, or at least I thought... which was the gateway to most of my demons... my thoughts gave them access. I talked about escapism earlier. I was comfortable with creating these places apart from reality. As I began to fantasize more and more, I realized that I would not only fantasize at night but then also during the day. Sometimes even in school. I would lie and say that my head was hurting so that I could lay my head on the desk but really, I had become way more interested in the parts of the "I do" "kiss the bride" and carrying over the threshold. I basically became this very, (I searched for another word but this was most appropriate) horny little girl and it all started with a kiss.

From that very first kiss I had turned my thoughts and attention away from the Lord and onto "Nella". He became the only guy I thought about. Day and night. Can I take a moment to show you how this teenage love started a continuous pattern in my male relationships? It was the same thing with Golden Man,

Superman, Nella and any other man I would date throughout the years. God took a backseat to them.

Eat and drink, saith he to thee;
but his heart is not with thee Pr. 23:7b (KJV)

I had taken God from His rightful place and erected an idol in His place.

"Teacher, which is the great commandment in the law?" Jesus said to him, "'You shall love the Lord your God with all your heart, with all your soul, and with all your mind." Matt 22:36-37 (NKJV).

I no longer longed for the presence of God. I longed for the presence of Nella. He had this infatuation with how he smelled. He played basketball. He said, that he couldn't stand that musty smell that all the other guys seemed to be ok with. He would often smell of anything "baby fresh" or "baby powder" scented. I longed for that aroma. I fantasized about his warm embrace, his lips touching mine and me having all of his big-headed babies. I desired to be one with this boy. I had plans that exceeded this moment in time. I saw a future with him. He would often confess that he saw one with me as well. All of these future plans, we acted out in our daily lives. We acted out in our daily decisions.

My apologies let me not speak for him, all of these plans I acted out daily. Remember in, "Turn The Tide," where I mentioned how the enemy can cause you to forfeit your own future by the decisions you'll make under his deception? Here's an example. Although small, deciding what to wear would be considered based upon whether or not I would see him that day. Where I would and would not go, depended on whether he would be there or not. These types of decisions should not be determined by man, but by God.

I still attended church every Sunday and Tuesday and Friday night. However, there were now walls up in my heart that kept God out of this particular area of my life. Walls that would take several years to come down. God could have my whole heart, is what I professed with my mouth. But the truth of the matter is that area, where I kept my affections, my deepest desires, where I kept love and unbridled lust for Nella, God couldn't have it. I protected this place. I kept this place for myself. I visited this place when my relationship with my mother was too hard to bear.

I kept this place to myself, yet the enemy somehow found himself a place within this place. We have to be honest with ourselves about our citizenship. Derek Prince makes this very plain in his book, *Pulling Down Strongholds*. Many Christians will indeed attest to there being a Kingdom of God, but would most likely hesitate in acknowledging that satan has a kingdom as well. He said, "If you are a citizen of the Kingdom of God through faith in Christ, you are automatically at war with the kingdom of Satan."

When we do not choose God, we inadvertently choose satan. I know that may seem "too real" for some people. I pray that you are not one of them. Because admitting this truth, is one of the first steps on the journey to becoming free from the bondages of satan. We cannot deal with the demons that we keep hidden. In deliverance ministry, you'll hear often "Up and Out" we must first EXPOSE satan for who he is, so that we may cast out those demons that like to hide themselves in our deepest most secret places.

One of my favorite scriptures says, "that you should show forth the praises of him who has called you out of darkness into his marvelous light:" 1Pt 2:9b (KJ2000).

Satan desires to keep you in darkness. But our wonderful Savior Jesus Christ, pulls us out of the darkness of deception and into divine truth. It is in His marvelous light that we experience true freedom.

In this darkness I had created a space for lust and perversion to live. We often think of perversion as abnormal sexual behavior. I'd like to, for the sake of exposing another layer of deception, (wow I see why the enemy hates truth bearers) broaden the definition of the word perversion. For the sake of truth, we will use this Google Dictionary definition, "the alteration of something from its original course, meaning, or state to a distortion or corruption of what was first intended." I like this definition because, although, perversion does often find itself in sexual connotations; it is also able to hide in the shadows of uncertainty.

For example, I would daydream about my future life, my future with my husband and a future family. God honors family. God promises us a future. He promises us a prosperous one as a matter of fact. But these fantasies were where I went to escape the broken pieces of my life. These places in my life, had the potential to make me stronger and I just wanted to hide. Well in my hiding place, my thoughts, the enemy took my thoughts of a beautiful family and future and altered them from their original course.

I began to have very explicit sexual thoughts and fantasies. I often fantasized about how I wanted our wedding night to "play out". Still I did not believe this was at all sin. Then, I became more interested in the details of the consummation. I would stay in that place for hours. With Nella being the center of my deepest affections, I wanted to share these things with him, these thoughts with him. But strangely I had even been deceived that these thoughts that included him, were only for me. I felt that I had to keep them in a secret place because it would change how people looked at me. I didn't want his image of me tainted. I was a good girl. A church girl and that's why he wanted me, so I had to do everything to maintain that good-girl perception.

I bottled all of these, now perverted, sexual desires up and hid them from everyone. This was the open door to one of the darkest and hardest areas of sin in my life, masturbation. I've been involved in many other things that some would categorize as way bigger on the scales of sin, however, this is one I have not spoken of until now. This was one that caused me to lie to even my closest of friends. I was so deeply embarrassed that I would actually take this "holier than thou" position towards the subject, even as my girlfriends and I would be in deep "home girl I've been there before" conversations. Shame and guilt would not even allow me to be transparent with those who I was in covenant relationship with.

The type of stronghold that this secret had on me, reminds me of those confessed by victims of child molestation. This secret grows up with you. You protect it. Yet the more you hide it, the more damage it does to your soul. You begin to go out of the way, to hide this big black hole in your soul. As it begins to eat away at who you are, you desire to fill it. But the only person who can fill this hole is Jesus, yet, He is the very person that we lock out of the secret place.

I want to pause here, because as the Lord begins to reveal hidden areas in our lives, depending on the level of vulnerability that this topic causes, you could be feeling quite exposed.

Take solace in knowing God also has a secret place. This is the place where you were formed. The enemy perverted it and created a counterfeit secret place. Satan's is a place where shame, guilt and condemnation happen. I found myself in a cycle of sin against my own body in this place. Because I found myself doing the thing that I didn't want to do, yet couldn't seem to control.

"Flee sexual immorality. Every sin that a man does is outside the body, but he who commits sexual immorality sins against his own body" 1 Cor. 6:18.

I do not understand what I do. For what I want to do I do not do, but what I hate I do (Rom 7:15 NIV).

It would be 5 years of this secret cycle of sin, before lust would scream out "this isn't ENOUGH"! By this time I had moved out of my mother's house. I was now living with a woman who saw the situation between my mother and I, who then adopted me into her family. Her family, who happened to be Muslim. By this point in my life and journey with Christ, I was all jacked up and feeling lost and confused. I felt rejected by my mother and did not identify it at the time. I felt as though my mother had chosen her addiction over her daughter. I share a story about this later.

But rejection and abandonment allowed me to run into the arms of another woman who positioned herself as the mother that I always needed and wanted. And in the moment, I thought it was beautiful. But as I have processed my experiences in life, this relationship pulled me away from Jesus Christ. I recall sharing in a Christian Missions class, that this was one of the loneliest periods of my life. I was void of my relationship with Jesus Christ.

I had left Him on the side of the curb, like a bike tossed, at the call of a child to come home for dinner. I tossed Jesus to the side and lost my ever-loving mind. Yes! I said it! I started drinking alcohol in school. I'd bring water bottles of vodka to school and because I was known as the Holy roller before now, security never checked my things. The only thing one of the security guards checked for was if I had my Bible. I guess I was being a light and didn't know it. I eventually did stop carrying my Bible in my backpack. Which was an outward sign of my inward struggles.

I understand now, why I responded to lust the way I did when it called out for more. I was void of the one person who, even in sin kept me anchored by His love.

I laid one night watching the movie "Love and Basketball". Both Nella and I played basketball for our High school teams. We still went to different schools, but we didn't see each other as often as you'd normally see your high school/childhood sweetheart. It's probably how our relationship lasted so many years actually.

April 2, 2002 many weeks of fantasizing had gone into the events of this particular day. Because we went to different schools, we had different break schedules. He decided that since he would be out of school that day, that I should come over to hang out. And in that moment, I decided that would be the day I answered lusts call. I planned out exactly how I would give this teenage boy, parading around as a full-grown man in my fantasies of him, my virginity. I meditated on it. Because I wanted it to be exactly as planned. The power of our thoughts is greater than we give credit to.

He wasn't a virgin. He'd lost his virginity pretty early, before we started dating. Which caused many insecurities in me throughout the course of our relationship. It is also good to understand, that spirits can be transferred through soul-ties. I never thought about why he'd had sex at such an early age or what types of demons he and his family dealt with. We often tImes don't as adults, it's hard to expect children to consider these things. That is why it is important to expose the devil by shedding light on our hidden and dark places, in order to become healed and whole.

April 2nd, I felt like all of the insecurities I had because of his sexual history, would go away. I didn't lose my virginity as most say. I gave it away, in exchange of the insecurities, the loneliness, the rejection all of it. Looking back, none of it went away. Sure, it was suppressed. I didn't feel alone. In all actuality I became super clingy. I couldn't breathe without saying his name. I didn't want to "do" life.

All I wanted was him and the closeness that sexual intercourse brought me. I substituted the closeness I was longing for from Christ, for this boy who I'd committed to spend the rest of my life with by now. In my head and heart of course. No natural wedding bells rang. But in the Spirit, I had come into a covenant relationship with him. And God, whose law is to put no other god before Him, was sadly nowhere to be found on the list of #1s. It was Nella and him alone that I wanted to feel oneness with.

Until we broke up a year later. I'd turned 18. My adopted mom worked on a university campus, I started noticing other guys who surprisingly made me feel the same way that Nella did. He was doing his thing at school and preparing for the near future, we broke up. Well… we left a door open for the possibility for the occasional sexual encounter to occur, but we agreed that I would go off to college a single lady.

As I found myself in bed with a guy I'd met on social media, on move-in day my first semester away at school. I thought, how stupid I was. I was very ashamed. I did indeed want to sleep with him and that's what I did. But the guilt I felt afterwards was what condemned me. This was just one of similar instances during my first year away at college. I remember getting on the phone with Nella and confessing all that I'd done. I just wanted to be back with him and back to the way things used to be. He'd been dating as well. He said, Dominoes we can't go back to those times, although just a year ago but you'll always have my heart. The next break for summer, I thirstily sought him out. I'm not sure if he was still dating his girlfriend, I didn't want to know. But that summer all we did when we met was have sex, as I would lay in his arms afterwards, I would now fantasize about my more innocent times of life. I needed that closeness and security that sex brought me, but I also longed for a place of purity.

I longed for this place of purity, but I kept doing the things which made me feel impure. Nella represented my innocence, as a result, I kept running to him over the years whenever things seemed unstable in my life. He'd always be there. As a matter of fact, many emails, texts and messengers he always made that very clear "I'm always here."

In the middle of writing this book the Lord spoke and instructed me to sever all cords with Nella. I hadn't had much contact with him in the last two years and out of the blue, I got a notification that we were now friends on Facebook. I didn't even remember sending a friend request, it had to have been a very old one. He started liking posts and pictures that I'd been posting and I can say, there was a nostalgic experience there. I actually reached out to my mentor, at the time, about what could possibly be there after being delivered from lust, promiscuity and loneliness. God had instructed me to sever all ties and I was feeling it hard to hit "unfriend". I did it, because living a completely submitted life means yielding to the voice and Spirit of God. I did it by faith. I acknowledge that there was still residue left concerning that soul-tie but I trusted that God would cleanse me completely of whatever it was.

Shortly after having done this, Nella, unexpectedly passed away. And I could clearly see the pain that God was protecting me from.

Mirror Mirror on The Wall:
Time to Reflect

By this point, a few words or feelings reocurred in my past; embarrassment, shame and guilt. These tools are some tricky tools that the enemy uses, but the word of God is most powerful over any lie of satan.

Guilt; is having committed an offense or crime.
We will be guilty of committing offenses against the law that God has placed before us.

However, God forgives us of our sins. If we confess our sins, He is faithful and just to forgive us *our* sins and to cleanse us from all unrighteousness. Its covered by the Blood of Jesus.

False guilt; When satan tells you, after you've confessed sin and been forgiven by God, that you simply have not been forgiven.

False guilt if meditated on long enough turns into shame. Think back to Adam and Eve. They were guilty of eating of the forbidden tree. But the meditation on what God would think of them, caused them to cover themselves in shame.

Shame causes us to [try] to cover ourselves. Embarrassment causes us to remain hidden. And what is hidden cannot be healed, it cannot be cast out, or dealt with properly.

The Bible informs us that we have authority over these types of thoughts in 2 Cor. 10:5 (NKJV),

"Casting down arguments and every high thing that exalts itself against the knowledge of God,
bringing every thought into captivity
to the obedience of Christ,"

Take time to meditate on this truth, according to the Word of God.

Chapter 6
Hello Beauty… Goodbye Brokenness

"STOLEN TREASURE"

October 29th 2017, was my mother's 50th birthday. The Lord woke me up with an encouraging message to share with her regarding righteous suffering. I had been spending lots of time in the book of Job as we studied it in my Survey of Old Testament class. I recalled a conversation that my mom and I once had where she revealed to me that she once believed her purpose on this earth was to only endure suffering. The morning of her birthday the Lord lead me to encourage her that her suffering although great, was not meant to break her for the sake of solely being broken but to break her for the sake of becoming beautiful.

This is how my day began and it was a precious moment between my mother and I. I also shared with her that in the enemy's attempt to keep us far apart from one another he revealed the power that we carried individually and collectively. My exact words were "The devil tried his best to take you away from me in more ways than one."

Until recently, I had not thought of sharing this story about the relationship between my mother and I in this book at all. However, a friend from school, asked me a question about how I was sure I'd been healed in a particular area of my life. The answer that I finally got around to is, you'll know when you can see the person or the situation with the heart of God and through His sight. You're healed when you view the situation in the manner that God views it. God will break you, to beautify you.

I'm reminded of Saul.

The men traveling with Saul stood there speechless; they heard the sound but did not see anyone. Saul got up from the ground, but when he opened his eyes he could see nothing. So they led him by the hand into Damascus. For three days he was blind and did not eat or drink anything (Acts 9:7-9).

Here was this man, Saul. Headed out on a journey minding his own business. He is struck by the Glory of God in the form of a bright light. He fell to the ground in the presence of this light. He was so affected by this light that he got up and could not see anything.

Have you ever felt that the Lord has interrupted a path, a journey or a plan that you were so confidently pursuing and knocked you down so hard that you felt as though you were lost? If not, I rest in the company of Paul, then Saul, because I feel that I've had this type of experience on a large scale at least twice in my life. Many more if you're talking smaller things like, my major in school or deciding on a career without consulting God first.

I believe it's important to stay here a bit with Saul because Saul had an agenda. He was on a journey to confront those who "were of the Way." He was headed to imprison and advocate death for those followers of Jesus. I can admit, this walk with Jesus is not for the faint of heart. I've been sought after simply because I proclaim my love and devotion to Christ Jesus. The same way that Saul set out persecuting Jesus and imprisoning His followers, so does the enemy set out to imprison and desires to deliver death unto us. My Apostle taught a sermon a while ago, about how we can become incarcerated by our memories. He said, "The greatest problem with your vision is your memory. Because memory fights against vision."

For many years after the death of my mother's first husband, I felt as though I had lost not one parent but two. I felt that although the only dad I'd known had passed away, that the most beautiful parts of my mother were also stolen from me. I don't think she's aware that this feeling started at such an early age in my life. I recall a joyous time of living with my mother. I remember her and I sharing laughs and doing girly stuff. I remember most of all, the feeling of never wanting to be away from my mother.

Once after we'd moved to Chicago she wanted to go out with friends, and she dropped me off to my grandma's house. I remember literally grabbing a hold of her leg, like I'd seen on television, but begging her not to leave. Nothing bad would happen to me at my grandmother's hands, this was a safe place, but I just remember always wanting to share space with my mother. This was actually one of those traumatic moments in my life where I cried out for my mother's love and affection and I felt my cries being rejected. She didn't push me off in a rough or aggressive way. But the struggle was happening internally, as I clung closer it was like she fought harder to pull me away. I couldn't express then, how I felt when she left. I felt angry. I felt like I was a problem and that I was in the way. I shared that I'd already experienced rejection earlier and this experience just fed it like steak and potatoes.

Some years later, my mother met a guy friend. Who introduced her to her pastime of gambling. Which later spiraled into addiction. Well, my mother has her own story to tell but she's told me how she's aware that the behavior was there way before the gambling came about. That the spirit of addiction had circled about her throughout other parts of her life.

I was eleven years old, I saw the problem with my limited vision and called it what it was. I actually found myself later writing about how I hated the man who introduced her to this lifestyle. Like a dope dealer, who hands out freebies, well aware that the recipient would be hooked and then leaves them there in the middle of this madness. I can admit that I had hatred in my heart towards this man that had stolen a part of my mother away from me. And for many years of my life, I was imprisoned by those memories, I lived there, and the spirit of bitterness grew in my heart and rage became a stronghold.

This story or series of stories are not meant to paint this horrible picture of my mother. However, I will not downplay the experiences that we had to go through in order to come out on the other side of victory. When my friend asked how I knew I was healed regrading my mother, I was able to say, "I see my mother in the way that God sees her." My mother and I, throughout my teenage years, experienced much strife and bitterness towards one another. I recall many times where I'd intentionally set out to hurt my mother. I wanted her to feel the same level of hurt that I'd experienced when I wanted my mother, but she'd be off and away gambling. I wanted her to hurt because I felt that she'd hurt me more times than I could count. I would make these declarations over us and our relationship. I did not know at the time that I was speaking word curses over our lives.

Once in a deliverance session at my church before returning to Chicago, as I lay on the altar purging and these roots of bitterness, rage and murder came out someone said, "You spoke a word curse over your mother when you were a child." I can be completely honest, I didn't know what this person was talking about, but the Holy Spirit had given him a Word of Knowledge and he came over and shared it with me. I needed to denounce that thing, that thought, that immature desire because it was the key to the devil causing all types of hell in mine and my mother's relationship even 20+ years later. I renounced the vow that I'd made and the curse that I'd spoken and then the work began… away from the altar.

Just as we discussed in the story "The Big Chop… again… and again" the physical casting out of the demons that were operating through me had come out, but because those demons had grown up with me, they had become a part of my personality. That spirit of rage as murder, would mask itself as passion. I remember times when I would become so angry if I felt injustice towards myself. If someone didn't keep their word to me, promised me something that they didn't follow through on, lied to me in any way or lied on me even. I've punched holes in walls. I've cut myself. I've also attempted suicide several times from feeling overwhelmed with the feeling of being a victim and not knowing how to break free from victimization. I was being held captive by my memories. I can identify that now. I could not even hope for a future because I was stuck on what happened in my past.

In "See Ya Lata Alligator", we discussed how the enemy is after our future. Here I was 31 years old and renouncing things that I'd spoken as a ten or eleven-year-old girl. I had not become free in my heart of the memories where I felt as though I was a victim, and no one came to my rescue. Which then exposed the position of my heart towards God. All these years where I'd felt like I was on fire for Christ I had not been fully in love with the Father God. I had actually blamed him for my suffering. I'd believed He had forsaken me.

For the director of music. To the tune of "The Doe of the Morning." A psalm of David.

My God, my God, why have you forsaken me? Why are you so far from saving me, so far from my cries of anguish? My God, I cry out by day, but you do not answer, by night, but I find no rest Ps. 22:1-2 (NIV)

I had been crying out to God as David longing for God to save me, feeling as though He was far from me. But the only distance between us was the distance I caused, He never left. He had become distance from me because of my heart. I did not love God the Father as Abba Father. He began to tell me how much He loves me and how He wanted me to know Him as Abba.

I went through many deliverance sessions. I feel like it was one every Sunday; and Monday through Saturday I would continue to be broken by the Father. Broken because I was this vessel molded from the clay that He'd placed on His wheel but before I'd completely formed in the fashion He desired for me, I was exposed to these experiences that started changing my shape, they allowed for impurities to become a part of who I would become and then I was shoved into the heat. I had to be broken because this vessel was not the one

God intended for me to be when He designed my future. I needed to be broken. We all do. We need to be broken by the Father in order for us to have the capacity to receive His love the way He intended for us to, not the way we've conceptualized His love.

"When I was a child, I talked like a child, I thought like a child, I reasoned like a child. When I became a man, I put the ways of childhood behind me. For now we see only a reflection as in a mirror; then we shall see face to face. Now I know in part; then I shall know fully, even as I am fully known"
1 Co 13:11-12 (NIV)

Mirror Mirror on The Wall:
Time to Reflect

One thing that blocks us from receiving deliverance is unforgiveness. Use this time to ask Holy Spirit to direct you to areas where you have not forgiven. This could be a person, place or thing. All of our past hurt does not happen at the hands of people. Places can represent a time of pain or hurt, and it is important to clear all blockages of unforgiveness out of the heart, if deliverance is truly what you desire.

"HIDDEN IN THE SHADOW"

I had this experience once, at my old church. We used to rent out a Seventh Day Adventist Church. There was a school attached. I used to go from the sanctuary to the kitchen often. And in between there was a gym. I used to shoot basketball before or after church sometimes.

One night after service I walked through the gym with a lunch bag in my hand. The lights were out but there was like one of those big flood lights right above the door. We are so used to having our shadows fall behind us that I had never noticed a shadow in front of me before. Maybe I had but this one was different.

As I looked in my shadow in front of me the shadow got bigger and it looked as though I was getting smaller.

I had prayed a prayer of being able to be used like Paul with God performing extraordinary miracles through me. In this shadow I began to see beyond the natural. I began to see, what I had asked God for. I began to see people being healed. The shadow got bigger and bigger and as it began to grow more and more people were being healed. I remember falling to my knees and weeping. I wept uncontrollably. I thanked God for this beautiful revelation. Because in this revelation I was able to see a glimpse of the future that God had in mind when He created me.

For many years, I'd thought that I was ignored, constantly overlooked, when in actuality I was, OVERSHADOWED. It took many years to realize the beauty in being overshadowed by the one who created me. We have become so accustomed to the world's definition of what it means to be overshadowed. Merriam-Webster says, "To cast a shadow over." It's as though there is always something or someone more important that causes the attention to be drawn away from us.

However, the beauty that I found in the shadows of The Most High God is incomparable. The word of God says,

"He who dwells in the secret place of the Most High
Shall abide under the shadow of the Almighty"
Ps 91:1 (KJV)

This world will have you afraid of the shadow, it will have you despising the shadow, and if that is not your testimony it is surely mine. I believed that it was not necessary to intentionally be seen, but I did not desire to go unnoticed either. I hated that place. I felt as though I was being used, taken advantage of and manipulated. And this was after I'd decided to whole-heartedly follow Christ. I felt like the place where God was keeping me was harming me. But this place was beautifying me. It was a quiet place where He stripped me down to nakedness, hidden from the criticism and judgment of others. This place was safe. And I needed safety for the level of vulnerability it took to bear my entire soul. Vulnerability was a very critical step of becoming healed *and* whole. Not just placing a bandage on a Boo-Boo but doing full-out surgery. Cutting out the old dead ways, thoughts, desires, attitudes, and ideologies etc. for His. For His everything. He cut me deep, in His shadow. But His shadow was a place of healing as well.

And He has made My mouth like a sharp sword; In the shadow of His hand He has hidden Me, And made Me a polished shaft; In His quiver He has hidden Me."
Isaiah 49:2 (NKJV)

It was in this shadow, the shadow of God where I learned of my "natural beauty". We hear this term a lot these days. Natural beauty is a fresh face, unmasked and clean. It is beauty, flaws and all. It is beauty in its original form. The shadow of the Most High God, my creator, allowed me to see myself the way He always envisioned me. Void of the impurities and falslflcations of satan's lying tongue. Void of any misconstrued perceptions of beauty that I myself, had in fact, placed upon my own image. Void of the word "natural", because the beauty God gives is SUPERnatural. It goes beyond human understanding.

"For the Lord does not see as man sees; for man looks at the outward appearance, but the Lord looks at the heart."
1 Sam 16:7b (NKJV)

Mirror Mirror on The Wall:
Time To Reflect

"You don't have a future,
until you can embrace your past...
He's healing the shadows of your life"

Apostle Dr. Matthew L. Stevenson III

As we conclude my life's stories, I pray that you were able to extract the spiritual lessons and apply them to your own life. I want you to take a moment and reflect on the quote above. When your past no longer causes you pain, but rather reveals certain aspects of your purpose, is how you know you've entered into a place of healing.

Take some additional space, if needed, to jot down your thoughts on this quote. What is your future saying? What has your past revealed? Are you still experiencing pain? Grief?

Be honest with yourself. Coupled with the other activities in this book, allow God to make you whole.

_____

_____

_____

_____

Conclusion

We talked about next steps of deliverance being to hate the devil that has you bound. My Apostle says often, in order for there to be a "struggle" with anything there has to be a motion of back and forth. One force pulling in one direction and the other in the opposite. It is in error when we say we are struggling with sin that we have not learned to hate. Because although our mouths have said that we don't want this life of sin, if there is no resistance then it is not a struggle. If it tugs and you follow then, you are not struggling with it. This book was not meant to only expose the devil, so that we can sit and reminisce with him. It is so that we expose his nature. Exposing his nature is the key to hating his schemes. If we come into a complete understanding that the enemy uses everything in his power to try to keep you from your God given purpose, prayerfully it will spark a hatred for those very tricks.

The beautiful thing about learning these tools, is that we are not left alone without instructions. We have the Bible. We also have Gifts of the Spirit. One of the main gifts operating through me as I write this book is the Gift of Discerning of Spirits. Another is the Gift of Wisdom. These two gifts are beautiful in that Holy Spirit desires that we know the things that He knows. He doesn't want to keep us in the dark. It is satan that thrives in darkness.

It is our heritage as Children of God to walk in His marvelous light. 1 Peter 2:9 (NKJV)

About The Author

Dominique D. Harris is currently pursuing her MDiv as a student at Trinity Evangelical Divinity School, a subsidiary of Trinity International University, in Deerfield, IL. She is a certified Evangelist, who enjoys the gift of one-on-one Evangelism. Sharing the gospel of Jesus Christ through discipleship, friendships and relationships has been the joy of Dominique's personal ministry.

As a former educator, Dominique has both the passion and burden of combating ignorance, by way of the Spirit of Truth. She is aware that it means nothing to have the solutions, if no one believes there is a problem. Therefore, she enjoys writing on topics in areas in which there has previously been an absence of truth surrounding the topics of:

- Christ Identity
- Deliverance
- Spiritual Warfare

As a spoken word artist and rapper, Dominique has the gifts and talent of an orator. However, presently God has called her to put ink to paper and although this is the first published book from this author, there are more to come very soon.

CONTACT

Website: www.dominiquedharris.com

Email: info@dominiquedharris.com

Facebook.com/iam.dominiquedharris

Instagram: @iam.dominiquedharris

Twitter:@iam_dominiqueh

www.ingramcontent.com/pod-product-compliance
Lightning Source LLC
Chambersburg PA
CBHW072153090426
42740CB00012B/2247